Ken Hom's Top 100 Stir-Fry Recipes

For Fung Sen Tsai with love, my Auntie 'Amu',
one of the greatest cooks I know

ken hom's top 100
STIR-FRY
recipes

Quick and easy dishes for every occasion

Contents

Introduction page 6

Beef page 10

Pork page 23

Lamb page 35

Poultry page 40

Fish and seafood page 64

Vegetable dishes page 88

Pasta, rice and noodles page 115

Basic recipes and Ingredients page 134

Index page 142

Introduction

Stir-frying is the most famous of all Chinese cooking techniques and it is also possibly the simplest, once you have all the ingredients prepared, measured out and immediately to hand, plus a good source of fierce heat. Its advantage is that, if done right, it enables foods to be cooked in minutes in very little oil, so they retain their natural flavours and textures. It is very important that stir-fried foods are not overcooked or made greasy.

Once you have mastered the technique, you will find that it becomes your favourite way of cooking. Stir-frying opens up endless possibilities for different combinations of foods and flavours. Using a wok is definitely an advantage, as the shape not only conducts the heat well but also enables you to toss the ingredients rapidly, keeping them constantly moving during cooking.

Once you have prepared all the ingredients for stir-frying, the steps are as follows:

• Heat the wok until it is very hot before adding the oil. This prevents the food from sticking and ensures an even heat. Groundnut (peanut) oil is my favourite precisely because it can take this heat without burning.

• Add the oil and, using a metal spatula or long-handled spoon, distribute it evenly over the surface. The oil should be very hot indeed – almost smoking – before you add the next ingredient, unless you are going to flavour it (see next point).

• If you are flavouring the oil with garlic, spring onions (scallions), ginger, dried red chilli pepper, or salt, do not wait for the oil to get so hot that it is almost smoking. If you do, these ingredients will burn and become bitter. Toss them quickly in the oil for a few seconds. In some recipes, these flavourings are then removed and discarded before cooking proceeds.

• Now add the ingredients as described in the recipe and proceed to stir-fry by tossing them over the surface of the wok with the metal spatula or long-handled spoon. If you are stir-frying meat, let each side rest for just a few seconds before continuing to stir. Keep moving the food from the centre of the wok to the sides. Stir-frying is a noisy business and is usually accompanied by quite a lot of splattering because of the high temperature at which the food must be cooked – hence my preference for a long-handled wok (see below right).

• Some stir-fries are thickened with a mixture of cornflour (cornstarch) and cold water, which must be thoroughly blended to a smooth paste. To avoid lumps in the sauce, be sure to remove the wok from the heat for a minute before you add the cornflour (cornstarch) mixture. It can then be returned to the heat in order to thicken the sauce.

Traditional Asian cooking equipment is not essential for stir-fries but there are some items that will make it very much easier. The most important thing is to have a good wok.

Wok

A most useful and versatile piece of equipment, a wok can be used not only for stir-frying but also for blanching, deep-frying and steaming. The shape permits fuel-efficient, quick, even heating and cooking. When stir-frying, the deep sides prevent the food from spilling over.

There are two basic types of wok, the traditional Cantonese version, with short, rounded handles on either side, and the *pau*, sometimes called the Peking wok, which has a single 30–35 cm (12–14 inch) long handle. The long-handled wok keeps you at a safe distance from being splashed by hot oil or water.

The standard, round-bottomed wok may only be used on gas cookers. Woks with flatter bases are now available, designed especially for electric stoves. Although this shape really defeats the purpose of the traditional wok, which is designed to concentrate intense heat at the centre, it is better than using an ordinary frying pan because it has deeper sides.

Choosing a wok Choose a large wok – preferably about 30–35 cm (12–14 inches) in diameter, with deep sides. It is easier and safer to cook a small batch of food in a large wok than a large quantity in a small one. Note that some modern woks are too shallow or flat-bottomed and thus no better than a frying pan. A heavier wok, preferably made of carbon steel, is superior to the lighter stainless-steel or aluminium type, which cannot take very high heat and tends to blacken, as well as scorch the food. Good non-stick carbon-steel woks that maintain the heat without sticking are now available. They need special care to prevent scratching but in recent years non-stick technology has improved, so that they can now be recommended.

Seasoning a wok All woks, except non-stick ones, should be seasoned before first use. Many need to be scrubbed as well, to remove the machine oil that is applied to the surface by the manufacturer to protect it in transit. This is the only time you will ever need to scrub your wok – unless you let it become rusty.

Scrub it with a cream cleanser and water to remove as much of the machine oil as possible. Then dry it and put it on the hob over a low heat. Add 2 tablespoons of cooking oil and, using a wad of kitchen paper, rub the oil over the inside of the wok until the entire surface is lightly coated. Heat the wok slowly for about 10–15 minutes and then wipe it thoroughly with more kitchen paper. The paper will become blackened. Repeat this process of coating, heating and wiping until the kitchen paper comes clean. Your wok will darken and become well-seasoned with use, which is a good sign.

Cleaning a wok Once your wok has been seasoned, you should never scrub it with soap or water. Just wash it in plain, clear water and dry it thoroughly after each use – putting the cleaned wok over a low heat for a minute of two should do the trick. If it does rust a bit, scrub it with a cream cleanser and re-season it.

Chopsticks

Chopsticks are used as a combination spoon and fork, and for stirring, beating, whipping and mixing. But, of course, you can also get along nicely with Western-style spoons, forks, ladles, spatulas and whisks.

Cleaver

To Chinese cooks, the cleaver is an all-purpose cutting instrument that makes all other knives redundant. Once you acquire some skill with a cleaver, you will see how it can be used on all types of foods to slice, dice, chop, fillet, shred, crush or whatever. In practice, most Chinese chefs rely upon three different sizes of cleaver – light, medium and heavy – to be used appropriately. Of course, you may use your own familiar kitchen knives instead, but if you decide to invest in a cleaver, choose a good-quality, stainless-steel model and keep it sharpened.

Whether you use a cleaver or a kitchen knife, the preparation of ingredients for stir-fries is vital – stir-fry cookery presupposes that every ingredient has been properly prepared for the cooking process. This means that meats and vegetables have been cut into appropriate shapes and sizes, so they will cook quickly and evenly while retaining their natural tastes and textures. Meat should always be sliced against the grain to break up the fibres and make it more tender when it is cooked. Vegetables should be sliced into a similar size and shape to the meat.

Spatula

A long-handled metal spatula, shaped rather like a small shovel, is ideal for scooping and tossing food in a wok. Alternatively, any good long-handled spoon can be used.

Notes for cooks in America, Australia and New Zealand

American and ANZ terms appear in brackets after ingredients in recipe introductions and ingredients lists where necessary.

All the recipes in this book list both metric and Imperial measurements. Conversions are approximate and have been rounded up or down. Follow one set of measurements only; do not mix the two.

Cup measurements, which are used by cooks in America and Australia, have been listed where necessary. You can also use kitchen scales to measure dry/solid ingredients.

Liquid measurements vary according to country, but remember that an American pint is only 16 fluid ounces whereas an Imperial pint is 20 fluid ounces. If in doubt, you may find this list useful:

2 fl oz (50 ml) = ¼ cup

4 fl oz (125 ml) = ½ cup

8 fl oz (250 ml) = 1 cup

16 fl oz (450 ml) = 1 US pint

1 UK/AUS pint (20 fl oz) (600 ml) = 2½ cups

1 teaspoon = 5 ml

1 tablespoon (UK/US) = 3 teaspoons = 15 ml

1 tablespoon (AUS) = 4 teaspoons = 20 ml

Note: tablespoon sizes in this book are UK/US, so Australian readers should measure 3 teaspoons where 1 tablespoon is specified.

1 Beef with Five Peppercorns

East meets West
Preparation time 30 minutes
Serves 4

450 g (1 lb) lean beef steak

3 tablespoons groundnut (peanut) oil

2 tablespoons cognac

100 g (4 oz) (½ cup) shallots, finely chopped

2 tablespoons five-peppercorn mixture, lightly crushed in a pestle and mortar or with the flat of a Chinese cleaver

½ teaspoon salt

250 ml (8 fl oz) Chicken Stock (see page 134)

25 g (1 oz) (2 tablespoons) butter, cut into small pieces

FOR THE MARINADE:

1 tablespoon light soy sauce

1 tablespoon Shaoxing rice wine or dry sherry

2 teaspoons cornflour (cornstarch)

2 teaspoons sesame oil

Steak au poivre is a popular French bistro dish that has fallen out of fashion recently. However, it is a dish that I have always enjoyed. In my version I like the mixture of five peppercorns, which is much more fragrant than using just one type.

The Chinese often find large pieces of beef intimidating, preferring to cut meat into slices and stir-fry it quickly, as in this recipe. The result is a fast dish that combines Fusion elements of East and West to give a unique slant on a classic. Serve with noodles.

1 Cut the beef into slices 5 cm (2 inches) long and 5 mm (¼ inch) thick, cutting against the grain. Put the beef in a bowl with all the marinade ingredients, mix well, and leave to marinate for about 20 minutes.

2 Heat a wok or large frying pan over a high heat until it is very hot. Add the oil and, when it is very hot and slightly smoking, remove the beef from the marinade with a slotted spoon. Add it to the pan and stir-fry for 2 minutes, until it is barely cooked. Remove and leave to drain in a colander or sieve set inside a bowl.

3 Pour out all the oil, re-heat the wok or pan over a high heat, then add the cognac. Deglaze by stirring and scraping the base of the pan with a wooden spoon.

4 Quickly add the shallots, peppercorns, salt and stock and simmer over a high heat until reduced by half. Stir in the butter, piece by piece.

5 Return the beef to the wok or pan and stir-fry for 30 seconds to warm it through. Serve at once.

2 Beef in Oyster Sauce

Classic Chinese
Preparation time 25 minutes
Serves 4

450 g (1 lb) lean beef steak

3 tablespoons groundnut (peanut) oil

3 tablespoons oyster sauce

1½ tablespoons finely chopped spring onions (scallions)

FOR THE MARINADE:

1 tablespoon light soy sauce

2 teaspoons sesame oil

1 tablespoon Shaoxing rice wine or dry sherry

2 teaspoons cornflour (cornstarch)

This was one of the most popular dishes in my family's restaurant. A good brand of oyster sauce does not taste at all fishy. Rather, it has a meaty flavour and goes very well with beef or pork. This dish is delicious served with plain steamed rice (see page 135).

1 Cut the beef into thin slices 5 cm (2 inches) long and put them in a bowl. Add all the marinade ingredients and mix well. Leave the beef to marinate for 20 minutes.

2 Heat a wok or large frying pan until it is very hot. Add the oil and, when it is very hot and slightly smoking, add the beef slices and stir-fry for 3–5 minutes, until they are lightly browned. Remove and drain well in a colander set inside a bowl. Discard the drained oil.

3 Wipe the wok or pan clean and re-heat it over a high heat. Add the oyster sauce and bring to a simmer. Return the drained beef slices to the pan and toss them thoroughly in the sauce. Turn the mixture on to a warm serving platter, garnish with the spring onions and serve at once.

3 Stir-fried Curry Beef

Informal supper
Preparation time 30 minutes
Serves 2–4

450 g (1 lb) lean beef steak

3 tablespoons groundnut (peanut) oil

225 g (8 oz) (1 cup) onions, sliced

2 tablespoons coarsely chopped garlic

1½ tablespoons finely chopped spring onions (scallions)

FOR THE MARINADE:

1 tablespoon light soy sauce

2 teaspoons sesame oil

1 tablespoon Shaoxing rice wine or dry sherry

2 teaspoons cornflour (cornstarch)

FOR THE CURRY SAUCE:

1 tablespoon Shaoxing rice wine or dry sherry

1 tablespoon Madras curry paste or powder

1 tablespoon dark soy sauce

1 tablespoon light soy sauce

1 teaspoon sugar

2 tablespoons Chicken Stock (see page 134) or water

Although curry is not a Chinese seasoning, it has nevertheless made its way into Chinese cuisine in a rather mild form. The hint of exotic spices adds a special, very subtle flavour to any Chinese dish. It works extremely well when beef is matched with vegetables. The best type of curry paste or powder to use is the Madras variety, which is the one favoured by most Chinese cooks.

This is a substantial dish that easily makes a filling meal for two or three. It may also be served as part of a multi-course, Chinese-style menu.

1 Cut the beef into slices 5 cm (2 inches) long and 5 mm (¼ inch) thick and put them into a bowl. Add all the marinade ingredients, mix well, and leave to marinate for 20 minutes.

2 Heat a wok or large frying pan until it is very hot. Add the groundnut oil and, when it is very hot and slightly smoking, add the beef slices and stir-fry for 3–5 minutes, until lightly browned. Remove and drain well in a colander set inside a bowl.

3 Wipe the wok or pan clean and re-heat it over a high heat. Add 1 tablespoon of the drained oil, then add the onions and garlic and stir-fry for 1 minute.

4 Add all the ingredients for the curry sauce, bring the mixture to a simmer and cook for 3 minutes. Return the drained beef slices to the wok or pan and toss them thoroughly with the sauce. Turn the mixture on to a warm serving platter, garnish with the spring onions and serve at once.

4 Beef with Ginger and Pineapple

Easy entertaining
Preparation time 30 minutes
Serves 4–6

450 g (1 lb) lean beef steak

225 g (8 oz) (4–6 thick slices) fresh pineapple

2 tablespoons groundnut (peanut) oil

2 tablespoons finely shredded fresh root ginger

2 red peppers (bell peppers), cut into wedges

2 spring onions (scallions), cut into 7.5-cm (3-inch) lengths

1 tablespoon water

2 teaspoons Shaoxing rice wine or dry sherry

1 teaspoon light soy sauce

2 teaspoons sesame oil

FOR THE MARINADE:

1 teaspoon salt

2 teaspoons Shaoxing rice wine or dry sherry

2 teaspoons sesame oil

1½ teaspoons cornflour (cornstarch)

This recipe is derived from the original I enjoyed at Yah Toh Heen (the former Lai Ching Heen), the marvellous Chinese restaurant in Hong Kong's InterContinental (formerly the Regent Hotel). I regard it as exemplary of the innovative New Hong Kong Cuisine, in which new ingredients and techniques are being employed to transform traditional recipes. A mouth-watering combination of tastes and textures, it is remarkably easy to prepare and is highly appropriate for a dinner party or any special meal. You can, if you wish, prepare the meat, vegetables and fruit in advance and store them, well wrapped, in the refrigerator until you are ready to cook.

1 Cut the beef into slices 5 cm (2 inches) long and 5 mm (¼ inch) thick and put them in a bowl. Add all the marinade ingredients, mix well and leave to marinate for 10 minutes.

2 Peel the pineapple and cut it into thick slices, discarding the tough core, then set aside.

3 Heat a wok or large frying pan, then pour in the groundnut oil. Add the beef and stir-fry for 3–5 minutes, until browned. Remove the beef with a slotted spoon and set aside.

4 Add the ginger, red peppers, and spring onions to the wok and stir-fry for 1 minute. Pour in the water, the rice wine or sherry and the soy sauce and cook for 3 minutes.

5 Drain the juices from the beef into the wok and add the pineapple. Return the beef to the wok and cook until it and the pineapple are heated through. Add the sesame oil and give the mixture one or two final stirs. Serve at once.

5 Savoury Beef with Asparagus

Informal supper
Preparation time 55 minutes
Serves 4

450 g (1 lb) lean beef steak

3 tablespoons groundnut (peanut) oil

100 g (4 oz) (½ cup) onions, thinly sliced

2 tablespoons coarsely chopped salted black beans

1½ tablespoons chopped garlic

2 teaspoons finely chopped fresh root ginger

450 g (1 lb) fresh asparagus, sliced on the diagonal into 7.5 cm (3 inch) lengths

3 tablespoons Chicken Stock (see page 134) or water

1 tablespoon Shaoxing rice wine or dry sherry

1½ teaspoons salt

½ teaspoon freshly ground black pepper

1 teaspoon sugar

2 tablespoons oyster sauce

FOR THE MARINADE:

2 teaspoons light soy sauce

2 teaspoons Shaoxing rice wine or dry sherry

2 teaspoons sesame oil

½ teaspoon each of salt and freshly ground black pepper

2 teaspoons cornflour (cornstarch)

Asparagus is the favourite vegetable of many lovers of good food. It is easy to see why. The cooked stalks combine crunchy and soft textures, subtle and distinct flavours. And in the late spring, when it is in season and readily available, it is not overly expensive. Asparagus can be combined well with almost any type of savoury food, but it goes uncommonly well with beef. Both of these main ingredients retain their flavours against the hearty black beans and garlic seasonings in this delicious and wholesome dish.

1 Put the beef in the freezer for 20 minutes. This will allow it to harden slightly for easier cutting. Then cut it into very thin slices 4 cm (1½ inches) long. Put the beef slices into a bowl, add all the marinade ingredients and mix well. Leave to marinate for about 15 minutes.

2 Heat a wok or large frying pan over a high heat until it is very hot. Add the oil and, when it is very hot and slightly smoking, add the beef and stir-fry for about 2 minutes. Remove the meat and drain it in a colander or sieve set inside a bowl.

3 Pour off all but 1½ tablespoons of the oil from the wok or pan and re-heat it over a high heat. Add the onions, black beans, garlic and ginger and stir-fry for 1 minute. Then add the asparagus and stir-fry for 1 minute.

4 Add the stock or water, rice wine or dry sherry, salt, pepper and sugar and stir-fry for 3 minutes or until the asparagus is slightly tender. Add more water if the mixture becomes too dry.

5 Quickly return the meat to the wok, add the oyster sauce and stir well. Turn the mixture on to a warm platter and serve at once.

6 Fragrant Beef with Peppers

Easy entertaining
Preparation time 40 minutes
Serves 4

450 g (1 lb) lean beef steak

3 fresh lemongrass stalks

3 tablespoons groundnut (peanut) oil

2 teaspoons finely chopped fresh root ginger

100 g (4 oz) (½ cup) shallots, thinly sliced

3 garlic cloves, thinly sliced

225 g (8 oz) red or green peppers (bell peppers) (about 1 large or 2 small), cut into 2.5 cm (1 inch) pieces

1 tablespoon light soy sauce

1½ tablespoons Shaoxing rice wine or dry sherry

½ teaspoon salt

½ teaspoon freshly ground black pepper

1½ teaspoons sugar

2 teaspoons sesame oil

FOR THE MARINADE:

1 tablespoon light soy sauce

1 tablespoon Shaoxing rice wine or dry sherry

2 teaspoons sesame oil

2 teaspoons cornflour (cornstarch)

My many trips to Thailand have led me to elevate lemongrass almost to the status enjoyed by garlic and ginger. It has a subtle but quite distinctive flavour that adds a certain something to the most prosaic recipes. Fortunately, it has now become generally available in most metropolitan areas in Western countries and it is well worth seeking out. Here, I have adapted the Thai version of this dish by pairing the lemongrass with sweet red or green peppers, which add colour as well as contrasting taste and texture.

1 Cut the beef into thin slices 5 cm (2 inches) long, cutting against the grain. Put it into a bowl together with all the marinade ingredients, mix well and leave to marinate for about 20 minutes.

2 Peel the lemongrass stalks to reveal the tender, whitish centre. Crush with the flat of a knife and cut into 5 cm (2 inch) pieces, then set aside.

3 Heat a wok or large frying pan over a high heat until it is very hot. Add the groundnut oil and, when it is very hot and slightly smoking, remove the beef from the marinade with a slotted spoon. Add it to the pan and stir-fry for 3–5 minutes, until browned. Remove and leave to drain in a colander or sieve set inside a bowl.

4 Pour off all but 1 tablespoon of the oil from the wok or pan. Re-heat over a high heat and then add the lemongrass, ginger, shallots and garlic and stir-fry for 20 seconds.

5 Add the peppers, soy sauce, rice wine or dry sherry, salt, pepper and sugar and continue to stir-fry for 3 minutes. Then return the beef to the wok and stir-fry for 4 minutes, mixing well. Drizzle in the sesame oil and give the mixture a few stirs. Transfer to a warm platter and serve at once.

7 Warm Vietnamese Beef Salad

Light and fresh
Preparation time 40 minutes
Serves 4–6

450 g (1 lb) lean, tender beef fillet

1 tablespoon fish sauce (*nam pla*)

1 tablespoon light soy sauce

1 teaspoon sugar

3 tablespoons groundnut (peanut) oil

5 tablespoons coarsely chopped garlic

225 g (8 oz) (2 cups) soft salad leaves

FOR THE DRESSING:

3 tablespoons white rice vinegar

1 tablespoon finely chopped garlic

2 teaspoons sesame oil

3 tablespoons groundnut (peanut) oil

6 tablespoons finely sliced shallots

salt and freshly ground black pepper

This is one of my favourite Vietnamese dishes. It has a clean, light flavour, and the stir-fried beef is paired with a freshly dressed green salad that is typical of dishes from tropical Vietnam. Although it is often served as a starter, I find it equally delicious as a main course in hot weather; simply double the quantities or add more salad.

1 First make the dressing: in a large salad bowl, combine the vinegar, garlic and some salt and pepper. Gradually beat in the sesame and groundnut oils, then stir in the shallots and set aside.

2 Cut the beef into slices 5 cm (2 inches) long and 5 mm (¼ inch) thick, slicing against the grain of the meat. Put the beef into a bowl together with the fish sauce, soy sauce, sugar and some black pepper. Mix well and leave to marinate for about 20 minutes.

3 Heat a wok or large frying pan over a high heat until it is very hot and add the groundnut oil. When it is hot, add the garlic and stir-fry for 20 seconds, until golden brown. Remove with a slotted spoon and drain on kitchen paper.

4 Reheat the oil and, when it is very hot and slightly smoking, add the beef to the wok and stir-fry for 2 minutes, until it is barely cooked. Remove it and leave to drain in a colander or sieve set inside a bowl.

5 Add the salad leaves to the dressing in the salad bowl and toss thoroughly. Arrange on a serving platter, garnish with the browned garlic and top with the warm beef. Serve at once.

8 Thai-style Chilli Beef

Hot and spicy
Preparation time 45 minutes
Serves 4

450 g (1 lb) lean beef steak

1 teaspoon salt

½ teaspoon freshly ground black pepper

1 teaspoon sesame oil

25 g (1 oz) (2 tablespoons) Chinese dried mushrooms

1½ tablespoons groundnut (peanut) oil

225 g (8 oz) (1 cup) onions, thinly sliced

2 tablespoons coarsely chopped garlic

4 red chilli peppers, deseeded and finely shredded

1 tablespoon Shaoxing rice wine or dry sherry

1 tablespoon oyster sauce

1 tablespoon light soy sauce

1 teaspoon sugar

3 tablespoons Chicken Stock (see page 134) or water

1½ tablespoons finely shredded spring onions (scallions)

Imitation being the sincerest form of flattery, this recipe is an admitted replica of one of the culinary creations of my good friend, Chalie Amatylakul. He is among the foremost authorities on Thai cookery and has taught me a considerable amount about the essentials of this great cuisine. With the exception of the fresh chilli peppers, it is quite similar to many Chinese stir-fried dishes. It is delightful, aromatic and quick to make. Serve with rice, as a main course, or with a vegetable dish.

1 Cut the beef into slices 5 cm (2 inches) long and 5 mm (¼ inch) thick, then shred them finely. In a bowl, combine the beef with the salt, pepper and sesame oil.

2 Soak the mushrooms in warm water for 20 minutes, then drain and squeeze out the excess liquid. Remove and discard the stems and shred the caps into thin strips.

3 Heat a wok or large frying pan until it is very hot. Add the groundnut oil and, when it is very hot and slightly smoking, add the onions and garlic. Stir-fry for 3 minutes.

4 Add the beef and chilli peppers and stir-fry for 2 minutes, then add the rice wine or dry sherry, oyster sauce, soy sauce, sugar and stock or water. Add the mushrooms and continue to stir-fry for 2 minutes, until the beef is thoroughly coated with the mixture.

5 Turn the mixture on to a serving platter, garnish it with the spring onions and serve at once.

9 Vietnamese-style Lemongrass Beef

Informal supper
Preparation time 70 minutes
Serves 4

450 g (1 lb) lean beef steak

3 tablespoons groundnut (peanut) oil

100 g (4 oz) (½ cup) onions, thinly sliced

2 fresh red or green chilli peppers, deseeded and coarsely chopped

3 tablespoons coarsely chopped garlic

1 tablespoon Shaoxing rice wine or dry sherry

2 teaspoons sugar

FOR THE MARINADE:

2 fresh lemongrass stalks

2 teaspoons fish sauce (*nam pla*)

2 teaspoons Shaoxing rice wine or dry sherry

2 teaspoons sesame oil

½ teaspoon salt

¼ teaspoon freshly ground black pepper

2 teaspoons cornflour (cornstarch)

TO GARNISH:

25 g (1 oz) (¼ cup) roasted peanuts, coarsely chopped

a handful of fresh coriander (cilantro) sprigs

Beef goes especially well with lemongrass in this Vietnamese-inspired recipe. The delicate citrus flavour complements the hearty beef. The garnish of roasted peanuts adds texture and crunch to this unusually aromatic dish, which you can serve with rice and a vegetable dish to create a complete meal.

1 Put the beef in the freezer for 20 minutes. This will allow it to harden slightly for easier cutting. Meanwhile, peel the lemongrass stalks to reveal the tender, whitish centre. Crush with the flat of a knife and cut into pieces 7.5 cm (3 inches) long.

2 Cut the beef into very thin slices, 4 cm (1½ inches) long. Put them into a bowl with all the marinade ingredients, including the lemongrass. Mix well and leave to marinate for 30 minutes.

3 Heat a wok or large frying pan over a high heat until it is very hot. Add the groundnut oil and, when it is very hot and slightly smoking, add the beef, plus the marinade, and stir-fry for about 2 minutes. Remove the meat and drain in a colander or sieve set inside a bowl.

4 Pour off all but 1½ tablespoons of the oil and reheat the wok or pan over a high heat. Add the onions, chilli peppers and garlic and stir-fry for 1 minute. Then add the rice wine or dry sherry and sugar and stir-fry for 3 minutes.

5 Quickly return the meat to the wok and continue to stir-fry for 2 minutes or until the beef is heated through. Turn the mixture on to a warm platter, garnish with the chopped peanuts and coriander and serve at once.

10 Beef with Orange

Classic Chinese
Preparation time 40 minutes
Serves 4

450 g (1 lb) lean beef steak

65 ml (2¹/₂ fl oz) groundnut (peanut) oil

2 dried red chilli peppers, cut in half lengthways

1 tablespoon dried orange peel, soaked and coarsely chopped (see page 138)

2 teaspoons whole Sichuan peppercorns, roasted and finely ground (optional) (see page 140)

1 tablespoon dark soy sauce

¹/₂ teaspoon salt

¹/₂ teaspoon freshly ground black pepper

1¹/₂ teaspoons sugar

2 teaspoons sesame oil

FOR THE MARINADE:

1 tablespoon dark soy sauce

1 tablespoon Shaoxing rice wine or dry sherry

1¹/₂ tablespoons finely chopped fresh root ginger

2 teaspoons cornflour (cornstarch)

2 teaspoons sesame oil

This is a dish from northern and western China. The Chinese always use dried peel – the older the skin, the more prized the flavour. It's easy to make your own dried peel but I have often made this dish with fresh orange peel and find that the tartness works just as well with the robust flavour of the beef. This is an easy dish to make and is a pleasant change of flavour from the usual stir-fried beef recipes.

1 Cut the beef into thin slices 5 cm (2 inches) long, cutting against the grain. Put the beef into a bowl, add all the marinade ingredients and mix well. Leave to marinate for about 20 minutes.

2 Heat a wok or large frying pan until it is very hot. Add the groundnut oil and, when it is very hot and slightly smoking, remove the beef from the marinade with a slotted spoon. Add it to the pan and stir-fry for 3–5 minutes or until browned. Remove and leave to drain in a colander or sieve set inside a bowl.

3 Pour off most of the oil from the wok or pan, leaving about 2 teaspoons. Reheat over a high heat, add the dried chilli peppers and stir-fry for 10 seconds.

4 Return the beef to the pan, add the rest of the ingredients and stir-fry for 4 minutes, mixing well. Serve at once.

11 Stir-fried Garlic Pork

Classic Chinese
Preparation time 30 minutes
Serves 4

450 g (1 lb) lean pork

2 tablespoons groundnut (peanut) oil

3 tablespoons finely chopped garlic

3 spring onions (scallions), thinly sliced on the diagonal

2 teaspoons chilli bean sauce

1 tablespoon light soy sauce

1 teaspoon Shaoxing rice wine or dry sherry

1 teaspoon sugar

1 tablespoon Chicken Stock (see page 134) or water

1 tablespoon sesame oil

FOR THE MARINADE:

1 tablespoon Shaoxing rice wine or dry sherry

1 tablespoon light soy sauce

2 teaspoons sesame oil

1 teaspoon cornflour (cornstarch)

Garlic and pork are two very familiar items in Chinese cuisine. Pork is the 'red meat' of Chinese cookery, since the lack of grazing land and pastures makes raising beef on a large scale impossible. Garlic is one of the three main spices (with ginger and soy sauce) in Chinese cuisine. The two ingredients go so well together, with the garlic nicely enhancing the fine qualities of the pork.

The black beans in this recipe are also important, giving the dish its trademark salty pungency. It is altogether very much a southern Chinese concoction, balancing crisp, clean, distinct flavours. My mother often made this dish and it has always been a favourite of mine. She would vary the taste once in a while by adding a dash of spicy chilli bean sauce. An easy dish to make in the wok, it goes perfectly with plain rice (see page 135) and any stir-fried vegetable.

1 Cut the pork into thin slices 5 cm (2 inches) long. Put the slices into a small bowl and mix them well with all the marinade ingredients. Leave to marinate for about 20 minutes.

2 Heat a wok or large frying pan and add half the groundnut oil. When it is very hot and almost smoking, lift the pork out of the marinade with a slotted spoon, put it in the wok and stir-fry quickly for 2–3 minutes. Remove from the wok and drain well.

3 Wipe the wok clean, reheat it and add the rest of the oil. Then quickly add the garlic, spring onions and chilli bean sauce. A few seconds later, add the rest of the ingredients. Bring to the boil, return the pork to the wok or pan and stir-fry for 5 minutes. Turn on to a warm platter and serve at once.

12 Spicy Pork with Fragrant Basil

Hot and spicy
Preparation time 10 minutes
Serves 2–4

1½ tablespoons groundnut (peanut) oil

3 tablespoons coarsely chopped garlic

3 tablespoons deseeded and finely chopped red chilli peppers

450 g (1 lb) minced (ground) pork

2 tablespoons finely chopped fresh coriander (cilantro)

2 tablespoons fish sauce (*nam pla*)

1 tablespoon oyster sauce

2 teaspoons sugar

150 ml (5 fl oz) Chicken Stock (see page 134)

a large handful of fresh basil leaves

This is a mouth-watering Thai-inspired dish. The minced pork is quickly stir-fried and tossed with so much fragrant basil that the herb almost plays the role of a green vegetable. Thai cookery, it seems, can never use too much basil. And here it is used to such good effect, helping to produce a marvellously aromatic dish that goes extremely well with plain rice. It is ideal for a quick but exotic family meal.

1 Heat a wok or large frying pan over a high heat and add the oil. When it is very hot and slightly smoking, add the garlic and chilli peppers and stir-fry for 30 seconds.

2 Add the pork and stir-fry for 3 minutes. Then add the coriander, fish sauce, oyster sauce, sugar and stock and continue to stir-fry for 3 minutes.

3 Add the basil and stir-fry for another minute. Turn on to a warm platter and serve at once.

13 Pork with Shrimp Paste

Informal supper
Preparation time 30 minutes
Serves 4

450 g (1 lb) pork fillet

1 teaspoon salt

1 tablespoon dark soy sauce

1½ tablespoons groundnut (peanut) oil

2 small, fresh red or green Thai chilli peppers, deseeded and chopped

2 small onions, coarsely chopped

2 tablespoons finely sliced shallots

2 tablespoons fish sauce (*nam pla*)

1 tablespoon light soy sauce

½ teaspoon freshly ground white pepper

1 teaspoon sugar

1½ teaspoons shrimp paste

a handful of fresh coriander (cilantro) leaves

In this dish, called *moo phad gapi*, tender pork fillet is marinated in dark soy sauce and flavoured with aromatic shrimp paste to make a special Thai treat. Serve with your favourite stir-fried vegetable dish and plain steamed rice (see page 135) for a satisfying meal.

1 Cut the pork into thin slices about 4 cm (1½ inches) long and place in a bowl. Add the salt and the dark soy sauce, mix well and leave to marinate for 20 minutes.

2 Heat a wok or large frying pan over a high heat until it is very hot, then add the oil. When it is very hot and slightly smoking, add the pork and stir-fry for about 2 minutes. Remove with a slotted spoon and drain in a colander or sieve set inside a bowl.

3 Quickly add the chilli peppers, onions and shallots to the wok and stir-fry for 2 minutes. Then add the fish sauce, light soy sauce, white pepper, sugar and shrimp paste.

4 Return the drained pork to the wok and stir-fry for 2 minutes or until it is cooked through. Add the coriander leaves, give the mixture a good stir and serve at once.

14 Stir-fried Pork with Spring Onions

Informal supper
Preparation time 20 minutes
Serves 3–4

450 g (1 lb) lean, boneless pork

1 tablespoon groundnut (peanut) oil

8 spring onions (scallions), cut on the diagonal into 5 cm (2 inch) lengths

1 teaspoon salt

½ teaspoon freshly ground black pepper

1 teaspoon sugar

FOR THE MARINADE:

1 tablespoon Shaoxing rice wine or dry sherry

1 tablespoon light soy sauce

2 teaspoons sesame oil

1 teaspoon cornflour (cornstarch)

This recipe illustrates the relative ease of using a wok. A basic stir-fried meat dish can be made in minutes. The key to success here is not to overcook the pork.

1 Cut the pork into thin slices 5 cm (2 inches) long. Put them into a bowl and mix in all the marinade ingredients. Leave for 10–15 minutes so that the pork absorbs the flavours of the marinade.

2 Heat a wok or large frying pan until very hot, then add the groundnut oil. When it is very hot and slightly smoking, add the pork slices and stir-fry for about 2 minutes, until brown. Remove the meat with a slotted spoon and leave to drain in a colander or sieve set inside a bowl.

3 Reheat the wok and add the spring onions, salt, pepper and sugar. Stir-fry for 2 minutes or until the spring onions have wilted. Return the pork to the wok and stir-fry for 2 minutes or until heated through. Serve at once.

15 Stir-fried Chilli Pork with Cashews

Easy entertaining
Preparation time 25 minutes
Serves 4

450 g (1 lb) lean, boneless pork chops

1½ tablespoons groundnut (peanut) oil

1 teaspoon salt

½ teaspoon freshly ground black pepper

4 tablespoons cashew nuts

1 tablespoon Shaoxing rice wine or dry sherry

1 tablespoon light soy sauce

1 tablespoon chilli bean sauce

2 teaspoons sugar

1 tablespoon finely chopped spring onions (scallions)

FOR THE MARINADE:

1 tablespoon Shaoxing rice wine or dry sherry

2 teaspoons light soy sauce

2 teaspoons sesame oil

1 teaspoon cornflour (cornstarch)

Pork, the preferred Chinese 'red meat', is delicious when combined with the taste and texture of nuts – in this case, cashews. A touch of chilli bean sauce is added for zest and you have a quick, savoury dish good enough to grace the centre of any family table. Serve with plain rice and a vegetable dish for a satisfying meal.

1 Cut the pork into thin slices 5 cm (2 inches) long. Put it into a bowl and mix in all the marinade ingredients. Leave for 10–15 minutes, so that the pork absorbs the flavours of the marinade.

2 Heat a wok or frying pan over a very high heat and add the oil. When it is very hot and slightly smoking, add the pork slices, salt and pepper and stir-fry for 2 minutes. Remove the pork with a slotted spoon.

3 Add the cashew nuts and stir-fry for 1 minute, then add all the rest of the ingredients except the spring onions. Return the pork to the wok or pan and stir-fry for 2 minutes. Garnish with the spring onions and serve at once.

16 Sichuan-style Pork with Peanuts

Classic Chinese
Preparation time 10 minutes
Serves 4

450 g (1 lb) lean boneless pork

1½ tablespoons groundnut (peanut) oil

1 dried red chilli pepper, split lengthways

6 tablespoons raw peanuts

FOR THE MARINADE:

1 tablespoon light soy sauce

2 teaspoons Shaoxing rice wine or dry sherry

1 teaspoon sesame oil

2 teaspoons cornflour (cornstarch)

FOR THE SAUCE:

2 tablespoons Chicken Stock (see page 134) or water

2 tablespoons Shaoxing rice wine or dry sherry

1 tablespoon dark soy sauce

2 teaspoons sugar

1 tablespoon chopped garlic

1½ tablespoons finely chopped spring onions (scallions)

2 teaspoons finely chopped fresh root ginger

1 tablespoon Chinese black rice vinegar (see page 141) or cider vinegar

1 teaspoon salt

1 teaspoon sesame oil

This is a pork version of a classic Sichuan Chinese dish that is usually made with chicken. It is quick and easy to prepare and is quite savoury – as is to be expected from any Sichuan recipe. The pork is robust enough to stand up to the various seasonings, while the peanuts add a wonderful textural quality to the dish. Serve with plain rice (see page 135) and another vegetable dish for a complete meal.

1 Cut the pork into 2.5 cm (1 inch) cubes and combine with the marinade ingredients in a bowl.

2 Heat a wok or large frying pan over a high heat. Add the groundnut oil and, when it is hot, add the chilli pepper and stir-fry for a few seconds (you may remove it when it turns black or leave it in; leaving it in will make the flavour stronger). Add the peanuts and stir-fry them for 1 minute. Remove the peanuts from the wok and set aside.

3 Lift the pork from the marinade with a slotted spoon, add to the wok and stir-fry for 3 minutes or until lightly browned. Remove the pork and drain in a colander or sieve set inside a bowl.

4 Wipe the wok clean and add all the sauce ingredients except the sesame oil. Bring to the boil and then reduce the heat. Return the pork to the wok and cook for about 2 minutes, mixing well all the time.

5 Finally, return the peanuts to the wok and add the sesame oil. Give the mixture a good stir and serve immediately.

17 Stir-fried Pork with Lychees

Light and fresh
Preparation time 10 minutes
Serves 4–6

450 g (1 lb) lean pork

2 teaspoons light soy sauce

2 teaspoons Shaoxing rice wine or dry sherry

1 teaspoon sesame oil

2 teaspoons cornflour (cornstarch)

225 g (8 oz) (1½ cups) fresh or canned lychees

1½ tablespoons groundnut (peanut) oil

2 tablespoons coarsely chopped garlic

2 tablespoons coarsely chopped spring onions (scallions)

In China, pork is almost always served as an accompaniment to non-meat foods. In this recipe it is paired with lychees. Try to use fresh ones: their tangy, grape-like flavour goes nicely with pork, at once complementing and contrasting with it. Serve over rice (see page 135).

1 Cut the pork into slices 5 cm (2 inches) long and 5 mm (¼ inch) thick and put them into a bowl. Add the soy sauce, rice wine or dry sherry, sesame oil and cornflour and mix well.

2 If you are using fresh lychees, peel them and remove the stones. If you are using canned lychees, drain off the liquid (which you will not need for this dish).

3 Heat a wok or large frying pan, add the groundnut oil and garlic and stir-fry for 10 seconds. Put in the pork and continue to stir-fry for about 2 minutes or until it is just cooked through.

4 Add the lychees and stir-fry for another 30 seconds to warm them through. Garnish with the chopped spring onions and serve at once.

18 Stir-fried Pork with Mushrooms

Informal supper
Preparation time 10 minutes
Serves 4

1 tablespoon groundnut (peanut) oil

3 tablespoons coarsely chopped garlic

2 tablespoons deseeded and finely chopped red chilli peppers

225 g (8 oz) minced (ground) pork

2 tablespoons finely chopped spring onions (scallions)

2 tablespoons light soy sauce

2 teaspoons sugar

3 tablespoons water

a large handful of fresh basil leaves

2 teaspoons sesame oil

FOR THE MUSHROOMS:

1 tablespoon groundnut (peanut) oil

225 g (8 oz) (2 cups) button mushrooms, sliced

1 tablespoon Shaoxing rice wine or dry sherry

salt and freshly ground black pepper to taste

This is a tasty dish that can easily be served with noodles or pasta. It combines savoury pork with mushrooms in an earthy, spicy mixture. Once made, it can easily be reheated.

1 Heat a wok or large frying pan over a high heat and add the groundnut oil. When it is very hot and slightly smoking, add the garlic and chilli peppers and stir-fry for 30 seconds. Then add the pork and stir-fry for 3 minutes.

2 Add the spring onions, soy sauce, sugar and water and stir-fry for 3 minutes. Then add the basil and stir-fry for another minute. Remove the mixture from the wok and set aside.

3 Wipe the wok clean and reheat it over a high heat. Add the groundnut oil and, when it is very hot and slightly smoking, add the mushrooms and stir-fry them for about a minute.

4 Add the rice wine or dry sherry and some salt and pepper and stir-fry for about 5 minutes, until the mushrooms are cooked through and have reabsorbed any remaining liquid.

5 Return the pork mixture to the wok, combine with the mushrooms and stir-fry for 2 minutes or until heated through. Just before serving, add the sesame oil and give the mixture a couple of quick stirs. Turn it on to a warm serving dish and serve at once.

19 Stir-fried Pork with Spinach

Classic Chinese
Preparation time 15 minutes
Serves 2–4

675 g (1½ lb) (6 cups) fresh spinach

450 g (1 lb) lean pork fillet

2 teaspoons light soy sauce

1 teaspoon Shaoxing rice wine or dry sherry

1 teaspoon sesame oil

2 teaspoons cornflour (cornstarch)

3 tablespoons groundnut (peanut) oil

2 tablespoons coarsely chopped garlic

1 tablespoon finely shredded fresh root ginger

1 teaspoon sugar

1 tablespoon light soy sauce

2 teaspoons dark soy sauce

2 tablespoons coarsely chopped spring onions (scallions)

salt and freshly ground black pepper

I love this simple dish, which my working mother used to make often. No wonder – it is not only tasty but healthy as well, and it was the only way she got me to eat spinach. The secret is to cook this dish in two stages: first the meat and then the spinach. This way, the meat does not stew in the spinach juices and get tough.

1 Wash the spinach thoroughly and remove all the stalks, leaving just the leaves. Set aside.

2 Slice the pork into 1 x 7.5 cm (½ x 3 inch) strips and combine them with the soy sauce, rice wine or dry sherry, sesame oil and cornflour in a bowl.

3 Heat a wok or large frying pan over a high heat until it is very hot. Add the groundnut oil. When it is very hot and slightly smoking, add the pork and stir-fry for 3 minutes, until browned. Drain immediately in a colander set inside a bowl, leaving 1 tablespoon of oil in the wok.

4 Reheat the wok. Add the garlic, ginger and some salt and pepper and stir-fry for 30 seconds. Then add the spinach and stir-fry for about 2 minutes to coat the spinach leaves thoroughly in the mixture.

5 When the spinach has wilted to about a third of its original volume, add the sugar, soy sauces and cooked pork. Stir-fry for 2 minutes, then transfer to a serving platter, garnish with the spring onions and serve at once.

20 Hunan-style Lamb

Hot and spicy
Preparation time 30 minutes
Serves 4

450 g (1 lb) lean lamb steak or fillet, or boned loin chops

1 tablespoon groundnut (peanut) oil

3 tablespoons finely chopped spring onions (scallions), white part only

6 garlic cloves, thinly sliced

2 teaspoons finely shredded fresh root ginger

1 tablespoon chilli bean sauce

1½ tablespoons hoisin sauce

1 teaspoon sugar

1 teaspoon sesame oil

FOR THE MARINADE:

1 tablespoon Shaoxing rice wine or dry sherry

2 teaspoons dark soy sauce

1 tablespoon light soy sauce

2 teaspoons sesame oil

1½ teaspoons cornflour (cornstarch)

Lamb is not a standard item on southern Chinese menus. It is much more common in northern and central China. The prejudice against lamb may be discerned in a southern saying: 'There are 72 ways of cooking lamb; most of them result in something quite unpalatable'. But this is unfair to lamb. As this recipe shows, it lends itself to imaginative uses. The most tender cuts, such as steaks and chops, are best for this dish.

Hunan (where Mao was born) is famous for its rather fiery cuisine. Chilli bean and hoisin sauces, as in this recipe, are among the spices most often employed. If you prefer something a bit milder than the hot Hunanese style, simply reduce the amount of chilli bean sauce. For a complete meal, serve with rice (see page 135) and a vegetable dish.

1 Cut the lamb into thin slices and put them into a bowl. Add all the marinade ingredients, mix well and leave to marinate for 20 minutes. Then drain off and reserve the marinade.

2 Heat a wok or large frying pan and add the groundnut oil. When it is very hot and slightly smoking, add the marinated lamb pieces with just a little of the reserved marinade. Stir-fry for 2 minutes.

3 Add the spring onions, garlic and ginger and stir-fry for 2 minutes longer. Add the chilli bean sauce, hoisin sauce and sugar and continue to stir-fry for 2 minutes.

4 Stir in the sesame oil, turn the mixture on to a warm serving platter and serve immediately.

21 Spicy Orange Lamb

Hot and spicy
Preparation time 35 minutes
Serves 4

450 g (1 lb) lean, boneless lamb chops

3 tablespoons groundnut (peanut) oil

1½ tablespoons finely chopped fresh root ginger

2 tablespoons thinly sliced garlic

1 tablespoon grated orange zest

1 teaspoon roasted Sichuan peppercorns, finely ground (optional) (see page 140)

2 tablespoons orange juice

1 tablespoon dark soy sauce

2 teaspoons chilli bean sauce

½ teaspoon salt

½ teaspoon freshly ground black pepper

1 teaspoon sugar

2 teaspoons sesame oil

FOR THE MARINADE:

1 tablespoon light soy sauce

2 teaspoons Shaoxing rice wine or dry sherry

1 teaspoon sesame oil

2 teaspoons cornflour (cornstarch)

Although the Chinese ordinarily do not like lamb, they have not tasted lamb in the West, where it is more delicate and subtle than the stronger-tasting version from China. Here I have combined the lamb with orange for a lovely contrast to the rich meat. The tartness of fresh orange zest balances the robust taste of the lamb beautifully. It is an easy dish to make and the spicy flavours add to its appeal. Serve with plain rice (see page 135) and vegetables for a wholesome meal.

1 Cut the lamb into thin slices 5 cm (2 inches) long, cutting against the grain. Put the lamb into a bowl with all the marinade ingredients, mix well and leave to marinate for about 20 minutes.

2 Heat a wok or large frying pan over a high heat until it is very hot. Add the groundnut oil and, when it is very hot and slightly smoking, remove the lamb from the marinade with a slotted spoon. Add to the pan and stir-fry for 2 minutes, until the lamb browns. Remove and leave to drain in a colander or sieve set inside a bowl.

3 Pour off all but about 2 teaspoons of the oil from the wok or pan. Reheat over a high heat and then add the ginger, garlic, orange zest and peppercorns. Stir-fry for 20 seconds.

4 Return the lamb to the pan, add the rest of the ingredients and stir-fry for 4 minutes, mixing well. Serve at once.

22 Lamb with Garlic

Informal supper
Preparation time 30 minutes
Serves 4

450 g (1 lb) lean lamb steak or fillet, or boned loin chops

1 tablespoon groundnut (peanut) oil

2 spring onions (scallions), white part only, finely chopped

6 garlic cloves, thinly sliced

2 teaspoons finely chopped fresh root ginger

1 teaspoon Sichuan peppercorns, roasted and freshly ground (see page 140)

FOR THE MARINADE:

1 tablespoon Shaoxing rice wine or dry sherry

2 teaspoons dark soy sauce

1 tablespoon light soy sauce

2 teaspoons sesame oil

1½ teaspoons cornflour (cornstarch)

Lamb is especially delicious when it is stir-fried. This way of preparing it with a lot of garlic and spring onions to balance its strong taste is a popular one. The most tender cuts of lamb, such as steaks or chops, are best for this dish. Serve with rice (see page 135).

1 Cut the lamb into thin slices and put it in a bowl. Mix in all the marinade ingredients and leave to marinate for 20 minutes. Then drain off the marinade and set the lamb aside.

2 Heat a wok or large frying pan until it is very hot. Add the groundnut oil and, when it is very hot and slightly smoking, add the marinated lamb pieces with just a little of the marinade. Stir-fry for 2 minutes.

3 Add the spring onions, garlic and ginger and stir-fry for 4 minutes. Turn on to a warm serving platter, sprinkle with the ground peppercorns and serve at once.

23 Hot and Tangy Minced Lamb

East meets West
Preparation time 15 minutes
Serves 4–6

1 tablespoon groundnut (peanut) oil

450 g (1 lb) minced (ground) lamb

3 tablespoons coarsely chopped garlic

2 tablespoons coarsely chopped fresh root ginger

2 tablespoons tomato paste

2 tablespoons sesame paste

1½ tablespoons dark soy sauce

1 tablespoon lemon juice

1 tablespoon chilli bean sauce

2 teaspoons sugar

1 tablespoon Shaoxing rice wine or dry sherry

This dish, in which the flavours of East and West meet, readily combines with pasta, rice, noodles or even bread to make an easy and substantial meal in less than 30 minutes. You can use minced beef instead of lamb, if you prefer. Sesame paste is a rich, thick, creamy brown paste made from roasted sesame seeds and should not be confused with the Middle Eastern tahini. If you cannot find sesame paste, use smooth peanut butter.

1 Heat a wok or large frying pan until very hot, then add the oil and lamb. Stir-fry for 2 minutes, then add the garlic and ginger and cook for 1 minute.

2 Stir in the tomato paste, sesame paste, soy sauce, lemon juice, chilli bean sauce, sugar and rice wine or sherry. (You will find it quicker if, as in this recipe, you are required to add a number of ingredients at the same time, you measure them together into a bowl and add them all at once.) Cook for 4 minutes, then serve.

24 Garlic Chicken with Cucumber

Light and fresh
Preparation time 30 minutes
Serves 4

450 g (1 lb) (about 2) cucumber

2 teaspoons salt

1 tablespoon groundnut (peanut) oil

450 g (1 lb) boneless, skinless chicken breasts, cut into 2.5 cm (1 inch) cubes

1½ tablespoons finely chopped garlic

1 tablespoon finely chopped spring onions (scallions)

1 tablespoon light soy sauce

1 tablespoon Shaoxing rice wine or dry sherry

2 teaspoons chilli bean sauce or chilli powder

2 teaspoons sesame oil

Cucumbers are rarely served raw in China; they are delicious cooked. In this recipe they are stir-fried with delicate chicken breasts and flavoured with garlic and chilli.

1 Peel the cucumber, halve it lengthways and remove the seeds with a teaspoon. Then cut it into 2.5 cm (1 inch) cubes, sprinkle with the salt and leave in a colander to drain for 20 minutes (this removes excess moisture). Rinse the cucumber cubes in cold running water and blot them dry with kitchen paper.

2 Heat a wok or large frying pan until it is very hot. Add the groundnut oil and, when it is very hot and slightly smoking, add the chicken and stir-fry for a few seconds.

3 Add all the remaining ingredients except the cucumber and stir-fry for 2 minutes. Now add the cucumber cubes and stir-fry for another 3 minutes. Serve at once.

25 Lemon Chicken

Classic Chinese
Preparation time 30 minutes
Serves 4

450 g (1 lb) boneless, skinless chicken breasts

300 ml (10 fl oz) groundnut (peanut) oil or water

2 tablespoons finely chopped spring onions (scallions)

FOR THE MARINADE:

1 egg white

1 teaspoon salt

1 teaspoon sesame oil

2 teaspoons cornflour (cornstarch)

FOR THE SAUCE:

65 ml (2½ fl oz) Chicken Stock (see page 134) or water

3 tablespoons lemon juice

1 tablespoon sugar

1 tablespoon light soy sauce

1½ tablespoons Shaoxing rice wine or dry sherry

1 tablespoon chopped garlic

2 dried red chilli peppers, halved

1 teaspoon cornflour (cornstarch), blended with 1 tablespoon water

2 teaspoons sesame oil

The southern Chinese have made a speciality of chicken cooked with lemon. Unlike many versions, which use a cloyingly sweet sauce, this recipe balances sweetness with tartness. Sometimes the lemon chicken is steamed but I think it is equally good stir-fried, especially if the chicken is 'velveted' beforehand by coating it with egg white and cornflour and pre-cooking it. Serve with plain steamed rice (see page 135).

1 Cut the chicken into thin strips about 7.5 cm (3 inches) long. Mix with all the marinade ingredients in a bowl, then refrigerate for about 20 minutes.

2 If using groundnut oil to cook the chicken, heat a wok or frying pan over a high heat and then add the oil. When it is very hot, remove the wok from the heat and immediately add the chicken pieces, stirring vigorously to prevent them sticking. After about 2 minutes, when the chicken pieces turn white, quickly drain them in a stainless-steel colander set in a bowl. Discard the oil.

3 If you use water instead of oil, bring it to the boil in a saucepan, then remove from the heat and immediately add the chicken pieces, stirring vigorously to prevent them sticking. After about 2 minutes, when the chicken pieces turn white, quickly drain them in a colander set in a bowl. Discard the water.

4 If you used a wok or pan, wipe it clean. Reheat it and add the stock or water, lemon juice, sugar, soy sauce, rice wine or dry sherry, garlic and chilli peppers. Bring the mixture to the boil over a high heat, then add the cornflour mixture and simmer for 1 minute. Add the chicken strips to the sauce and stir-fry them just long enough to coat them all with the sauce. Stir in the sesame oil and mix once again. Then turn on to a warm serving platter, garnish with the spring onions and serve at once.

41

26 Stir-fried Chicken with Grilled Peppers

East meets West
Preparation time 40 minutes
Serves 4

4 peppers (bell peppers), a mixture of red, yellow and green

2 tablespoons extra virgin olive oil

450 g (1 lb) boneless, skinless chicken breasts

300 ml (10 fl oz) groundnut (peanut) oil or water

1 tablespoon groundnut (peanut) oil

2 tablespoons finely sliced garlic

150 ml (5 fl oz) Chicken Stock (see page 134)

2 teaspoons chilli bean sauce

2 teaspoons sugar

1½ tablespoons Shaoxing rice wine or dry sherry

1 tablespoon light soy sauce

1 teaspoon cornflour (cornstarch), blended with 1 tablespoon water

FOR THE MARINADE:

1 egg white

1 teaspoon salt

2 teaspoons cornflour (cornstarch)

As a student living in southern France, I discovered the taste of grilled or roasted peppers. Cooked over an open flame on a stove or barbecue, the peppers acquire an exquisitely sweet, smoky flavour. Serve with rice (see page 135).

1 Using tongs, hold each pepper directly over a gas flame or grill (broiler) and cook until the skin has blackened all over. If you don't have a gas stove, put them under a hot grill (broiler), turning occasionally, until blackened. Place in a plastic bag and close it tightly. When the peppers have cooled, remove from the bag and peel off the charred skin. Clean the insides and discard the seeds. Cut the peppers into long strips, drizzle them with the olive oil and set aside.

2 Cut the chicken into 2.5 cm (1 inch) cubes. Mix with all the marinade ingredients in a small bowl, then refrigerate for about 20 minutes.

3 If using groundnut oil to cook the chicken, heat a wok or large frying pan over a high heat and add the oil. When it is very hot, remove the wok or pan from the heat and immediately add the chicken pieces, stirring vigorously to prevent them sticking. When they turn white, after about 2 minutes, quickly drain the chicken in a stainless-steel colander set in a bowl. Discard the oil.

4 If you use water instead of oil, bring it to the boil in a saucepan, then remove from the heat and immediately add the chicken pieces, stirring vigorously to prevent them sticking. When the chicken pieces turn white, after about 2 minutes, quickly drain them in a colander set in a bowl. Discard the water.

5 If you used a wok or pan, wipe it clean. Reheat it until it is very hot, then add the tablespoon of groundnut oil. When it is very hot, add the garlic slices and stir-fry for 2 minutes, until golden brown.

6 Add the stock, chilli bean sauce, sugar, rice wine or sherry and soy sauce. Cook for 2 minutes, then add the cornflour and water mixture and cook for 20 seconds.

7 Add the chicken and the roasted pepper strips and stir-fry for another 2 minutes, coating the chicken thoroughly with the sauce. Serve at once.

27 Spicy Chicken with Mint

Light and fresh
Preparation time 30 minutes
Serves 4

450 g (1 lb) boneless, skinless chicken breasts

300 ml (10 fl oz) groundnut (peanut) oil or water

1 tablespoon groundnut (peanut) oil

225 g (8 oz) (2 cups) red or green peppers (bell peppers), cut into 2.5 cm (1 inch) dice

1 tablespoon thinly sliced garlic

150 ml (5 fl oz) Chicken Stock (see page 134)

1½ tablespoons Madras curry paste

2 teaspoons chilli bean sauce

2 teaspoons sugar

1½ tablespoons Shaoxing rice wine or dry sherry

1 tablespoon light soy sauce

1 teaspoon cornflour (cornstarch), blended with 1 tablespoon water

8 fresh mint leaves

FOR THE MARINADE:

1 egg white

1 teaspoon salt

2 teaspoons cornflour (cornstarch)

Here is a lovely, spicy chicken dish with fresh mint as a counterbalance. If you grow your own mint, it is likely to be even more delicate and subtle than anything you can buy. Mint is probably the most widely used of all the aromatic herbs and the one most readily accessible.

A touch of curry is used with the chilli bean sauce to give this dish a real kick. The chicken is 'velveted' to preserve its succulence and flavour. You can use the traditional oil method or, for a less fattening version, substitute water. The peppers provide a crunchy texture that makes a wonderful complement to the soft, tender chicken. Serve with plain steamed rice (see page 135) and a salad.

1 Cut the chicken breasts into 2.5 cm (1 inch) cubes. Mix with all the marinade ingredients in a small bowl and refrigerate for 20 minutes.

2 If cooking the chicken in groundnut oil, heat a wok or frying pan over a high heat and then add the oil. When it is very hot, remove the wok from the heat and immediately add the chicken pieces, stirring vigorously to prevent them sticking. After about 2 minutes, when the chicken pieces turn white, quickly drain them in a stainless-steel colander set in a bowl. Discard the oil.

3 If you use water instead of oil, bring it to the boil in a saucepan, then remove from the heat and immediately add the chicken pieces, stirring vigorously to prevent them sticking. After about 2 minutes, when the chicken pieces turn white, quickly drain them in a colander set in a bowl. Discard the water.

4 If you used a wok or pan, wipe it clean. Heat it over a high heat, then add the tablespoon of oil. When it is very hot, add the peppers and garlic and stir-fry for 2 minutes.

5 Add all the remaining ingredients except the cornflour mixture and mint leaves and cook for 2 minutes. Add the cornflour mixture and cook for 20 seconds, stirring, then add the drained chicken and stir-fry for another 2 minutes, coating the chicken thoroughly with the sauce.

6 Finally add the mint leaves and stir for 1 minute to mix well. Turn on to a warm platter and serve at once.

28 Walnut Chicken

Informal supper
Preparation time 30 minutes
Serves 4

450 g (1 lb) boneless, skinless chicken breasts

75 g (3 oz) (⅓ cup) shelled walnut halves or pieces

300 ml (10 fl oz) groundnut (peanut) oil or water

1 tablespoon groundnut (peanut) oil

2 teaspoons finely chopped garlic

1 teaspoon finely chopped fresh root ginger

2 tablespoons finely chopped spring onions (scallions)

2 tablespoons Shaoxing rice wine or dry sherry

1½ tablespoons light soy sauce

FOR THE MARINADE:

1 egg white

1 teaspoon salt

2 teaspoons cornflour (cornstarch)

This recipe pairs the crunchy texture of walnuts with the softness of chicken in a classic stir-fry dish. For a variation, try using other nuts, such as pine nuts or almonds, but make sure they are very fresh. Stale nuts tend to go soft and will ruin both the texture and the flavour of the dish.

1 Cut the chicken breasts into 2.5 cm (1 inch) cubes. Mix them with all the marinade ingredients in a small bowl and refrigerate for about 20 minutes.

2 Blanch the walnuts in a small pan of boiling water for 5 minutes, then drain.

3 If using groundnut oil to cook the chicken, heat a wok or frying pan over a high heat and then add the oil. When it is very hot, remove the wok from the heat and immediately add the chicken pieces, stirring vigorously to prevent them sticking. After about 2 minutes, when the chicken pieces turn white, quickly drain them in a stainless-steel colander set in a bowl. Discard the oil.

4 If you use water instead of oil, bring it to the boil in a saucepan, then remove from the heat and immediately add the chicken pieces, stirring vigorously to prevent them sticking. After about 2 minutes, when the chicken pieces turn white, quickly drain them in a colander set in a bowl. Discard the water.

5 If you used a wok or pan, wipe it clean. Heat it over a high heat, then add the tablespoon of oil. Add the walnuts and stir-fry for 1 minute, then remove from the pan and set aside.

6 Add the garlic, ginger and spring onions to the pan and stir-fry for a few seconds. Return the walnuts to the pan and then add the rice wine or dry sherry and the soy sauce. Add the chicken to the wok and stir-fry the mixture for 2 minutes. Serve at once.

29 Shredded Chicken with Sesame Seeds

Hot and spicy
Preparation time 30 minutes
Serves 3–4

450 g (1 lb) boneless, skinless chicken breasts

300 ml (10 fl oz) groundnut (peanut) oil or water

1 tablespoon groundnut (peanut) oil

1 tablespoon white sesame seeds

FOR THE MARINADE:

1 egg white

½ teaspoon salt

2 teaspoons cornflour (cornstarch)

FOR THE SAUCE:

2 teaspoons dark soy sauce

2 teaspoons Chinese black rice vinegar or cider vinegar

2 teaspoons chilli bean sauce

2 teaspoons sesame oil

2 teaspoons sugar

1 tablespoon Shaoxing rice wine or dry sherry

1 teaspoon whole Sichuan peppercorns, roasted (see page 140)

1½ tablespoons finely chopped spring onions (scallions)

This is my version of a fragrant Sichuan dish popularly known as 'Strange Taste Chicken' because it incorporates so many flavours, being hot, spicy, sour, sweet and salty all at the same time. It is delicious served hot but I find it makes an excellent cold dish as well. I simply let it cool and serve it at room temperature. The sesame seeds add a crunchy texture that contrasts nicely with the tender chicken.

1 Cut the chicken breasts into strips about 7.5 cm (3 inches) long. Mix with all the marinade ingredients in a small bowl and refrigerate for about 20 minutes.

2 If using groundnut oil to cook the chicken, heat a wok or frying pan over a high heat and then add the oil. When it is very hot, remove the wok from the heat and immediately add the chicken pieces, stirring vigorously to prevent them sticking. After about 2 minutes, when the chicken pieces turn white, quickly drain them in a stainless-steel colander set in a bowl. Discard the oil.

3 If you use water instead of oil, bring it to the boil in a saucepan, then remove from the heat and immediately add the chicken pieces, stirring vigorously to prevent them sticking. After about 2 minutes, when the chicken pieces turn white, quickly drain them in a colander set in a bowl. Discard the water.

4 If you used a wok or pan, wipe it clean. Heat it until it is very hot, then add the tablespoon of oil. Immediately add the sesame seeds and stir-fry for 30 seconds or until they are slightly brown.

5 Add all the sauce ingredients and bring to the boil. Return the cooked chicken to the pan and stir-fry the mixture for another 2 minutes, coating the pieces thoroughly with the sauce and sesame seeds. Serve at once or let it cool and serve at room temperature.

30 Broccoli Chicken

Informal supper
Preparation time 50 minutes
Serves 4

450 g (1 lb) (2 heads) broccoli

450 g (1 lb) boneless, skinless chicken thighs

cornflour (cornstarch), for dusting

400 ml (14 fl oz) groundnut (peanut) oil, plus 1 tablespoon

3 tablespoons coarsely chopped garlic

1 small onion, quartered

2 tablespoons Shaoxing rice wine or dry sherry

3 tablespoons water or Chicken Stock (see page 134)

2 medium tomatoes, quartered

3 tablespoons oyster sauce

2 tablespoons Thai fish sauce (*nam pla*)

1 teaspoon sugar

1 teaspoon salt

½ teaspoon freshly ground black pepper

2 teaspoons sesame oil

FOR THE MARINADE:

½ teaspoon freshly ground black pepper

1 tablespoon Thai fish sauce (*nam pla*)

1 teaspoon light soy sauce

Chicken and broccoli are a wonderful combination. In this Vietnamese-inspired recipe, the chicken is first marinated, then fried, before being paired with crunchy green broccoli. In Vietnam, Chinese broccoli, which is slightly more woody and bitter, would be used. But here I use the variety found in the West, which is sweeter, with a distinctive, mild flavour. Chicken thighs are used because of their robust taste, which holds up well to the frying. Serve with rice (see page 135) and a vegetable dish for a wholesome meal.

1 Separate the broccoli heads into small florets and peel and slice the stems. Blanch the broccoli pieces in a large pan of boiling salted water for 2–3 minutes, then drain and immerse in cold water. Drain again thoroughly.

2 Cut the chicken into 2.5 cm (1 inch) pieces and combine them with the marinade ingredients. Mix well and leave to marinate for 30 minutes. Dust the chicken pieces with cornflour, shaking off any excess.

3 Heat a wok or large frying pan over a high heat and add the 400 ml (14 fl oz) oil. When it is very hot and slightly smoking, deep-fry the chicken pieces for 8 minutes or until they are golden brown. Remove with a slotted spoon and drain on kitchen paper. You may have to do this in 2 or more batches.

4 Drain off all the oil, reheat the wok and add the tablespoon of oil. When it is hot, add the garlic and onion and stir-fry for 1 minute. Then add the blanched broccoli and stir-fry for 1 minute longer. Add the Shaoxing rice wine or dry sherry and water or stock and stir-fry over a moderate to high heat for 4 minutes, until the broccoli is thoroughly heated through.

5 Add the tomatoes, oyster sauce, fish sauce, sugar, salt, pepper and sesame oil and stir-fry for 30 seconds. Then add the drained chicken and stir-fry for 2 minutes, until the chicken is thoroughly heated through. Transfer to a warm platter and serve at once.

31 Thai-style Ginger Chicken

Easy entertaining
Preparation time 45 minutes
Serves 4

450 g (1 lb) boneless, skinless chicken thighs

1 tablespoon Chinese dried wood ears

1 tablespoon groundnut (peanut) oil

1 small onion, cut into 8 wedges

2 tablespoons coarsely chopped garlic

4 tablespoons finely shredded fresh root ginger

1 tablespoon yellow bean sauce

2 teaspoons sugar

1 teaspoon salt

2 tablespoons Shaoxing rice wine or dry sherry

3 tablespoons finely shredded spring onions (scallions)

FOR THE MARINADE:

2 teaspoons light soy sauce

1 teaspoon dark soy sauce

1 tablespoon Shaoxing rice wine or dry sherry

$\frac{1}{2}$ teaspoon salt

$\frac{1}{2}$ teaspoon freshly ground black pepper

1 teaspoon sesame oil

2 teaspoons cornflour (cornstarch)

This Thai-inspired recipe is an extremely close relative of a Chinese one. Contrary to what most people think, not all Thai dishes include chilli peppers and taste spicy. Many of the Thais who have Chinese ancestry come from southern China and their cooking reflects their roots – that is, subtle cooking with nuances, rather than the strong, assertive chilli flavour that characterises much of Thai cooking. This dish is delicious with plain rice (see page 135).

1 Cut the chicken into 5 cm (2 inch) chunks and place in a bowl. Mix together all the marinade ingredients except the cornflour and pour them over the chicken. Then mix in the cornflour until all the chicken pieces are thoroughly coated. Leave to marinate for about 30 minutes, then drain the chicken and discard the marinade.

2 Soak the dried wood ears in warm water for about 20 minutes, until soft. Drain and rinse in cold water, then cut off any hard bits. Shred the wood ears finely.

3 Heat a wok or large frying pan over a high heat and add the groundnut oil. When it is very hot and slightly smoking, add the chicken and stir-fry for 5 minutes, until it begins to brown. Remove the chicken and drain.

4 Pour off all but 1 tablespoon of oil from the wok. Add the onion, garlic, ginger and wood ears and stir-fry for 1 minute. Then add the yellow bean sauce, sugar and salt and continue to stir-fry for 30 seconds.

5 Return the chicken to the wok and stir-fry for 4 minutes. Finally, add the rice wine or dry sherry and stir-fry for 2 minutes or until the chicken is cooked through. Garnish with the spring onions and serve.

32 Chicken with Black Bean Sauce

Classic Chinese
Preparation time 15 minutes
Serves 4

450 g (1 lb) boneless, skinless chicken breasts

1 tablespoon light soy sauce

1½ tablespoons Shaoxing rice wine or dry sherry

½ teaspoon salt

1 teaspoon sugar

1 teaspoon sesame oil

2 teaspoons cornflour (cornstarch)

2 tablespoons groundnut (peanut) oil

1 tablespoon finely chopped fresh root ginger

1½ tablespoons coarsely chopped garlic

2 tablespoons finely chopped shallots

3½ tablespoons finely chopped spring onions (scallions)

2½ tablespoons coarsely chopped salted black beans

150 ml (5 fl oz) Chicken Stock (see page 134)

This is a favourite of many first-time diners in Chinese restaurants, and no wonder. The fragrance of fermented black bean sauce mixed with garlic and ginger is mouth-watering. It can be cooked ahead of time and reheated, and it is also delicious served cold.

1 Cut the chicken into 5 cm (2 inch) chunks and place in a bowl. Mix with the soy sauce, rice wine or sherry, salt, sugar, sesame oil and cornflour.

2 Heat a wok over a high heat, then add the groundnut oil. When it is very hot and slightly smoking, add the chicken and stir-fry for 2 minutes.

3 Add the ginger, garlic, shallots, 1½ tablespoons of the spring onions and the black beans and stir-fry for 2 minutes.

4 Add the stock, bring the mixture to the boil, then reduce the heat. Cover and simmer for 3 minutes or until the chicken is cooked. Garnish with the remaining spring onions and serve.

33 Quick Orange and Lemon Chicken

Light and fresh
Preparation time 20 minutes
Serves 2–4

450 g (1 lb) boneless, skinless chicken breasts

1 tablespoon groundnut (peanut) oil

1 teaspoon salt

2 tablespoons finely grated orange zest

1 tablespoon finely grated lemon zest

2 teaspoons sesame oil

3 tablespoons finely chopped fresh coriander (cilantro)

freshly ground white pepper

FOR THE MARINADE:

2 teaspoons light soy sauce

1 teaspoon Shaoxing rice wine or dry sherry

1 teaspoon cornflour (cornstarch)

Nothing could be quicker and tastier than this simple dish, stir-fried in a hot wok. The tangy flavours of orange and lemon zest give the chicken a new dimension. It is easy to prepare and takes literally minutes to cook.

1 Cut the chicken breasts into 2.5 cm (1 inch) cubes. Combine them with the marinade ingredients in a small bowl and refrigerate for about 15 minutes.

2 Heat a wok until it is very hot and then add the oil. When the oil is very hot and slightly smoking, add the chicken, together with the salt, orange and lemon zest and some pepper. Stir-fry for 4 minutes or until the chicken is cooked.

3 Stir in the sesame oil, give the mixture a couple of turns and cook for 3 minutes. Finally, add the coriander and stir-fry for another minute. Turn on to a platter and serve at once.

34 Chicken with Chilli Peppers and Basil

| Easy entertaining |
| Preparation time 10 minutes |
| Serves 4 |

2 tablespoons groundnut (peanut) oil

450 g (1 lb) boneless, skinless chicken thighs, cut into 2.5 cm (1 inch) pieces

3 tablespoons finely sliced shallots

3 tablespoons chopped garlic

3 fresh red or green Thai chilli peppers, deseeded and finely shredded

2 tablespoons fish sauce (*nam pla*)

2 teaspoons dark soy sauce

2 teaspoons sugar

a large handful of basil leaves

This traditional dish, called *gai phad bai krapao*, is very easy to prepare. Although ordinary fresh basil is fine, if you can find Thai basil, its unique, pungent aroma makes the dish especially mouth-watering.

1 Heat a wok or large frying pan until it is very hot, then add 1 tablespoon of the oil. When it is very hot, add the chicken and stir-fry over a high heat for 8 minutes, until browned all over. Using a slotted spoon, transfer the chicken to a colander or sieve to drain.

2 Reheat the wok and add the remaining oil. Toss in the shallots and garlic and stir-fry for 3 minutes, until they are golden brown.

3 Return the chicken to the wok and add the chilli peppers, fish sauce, dark soy sauce and sugar. Stir-fry over a high heat for 8 minutes or until the chicken is cooked through. Stir in the basil leaves and serve at once.

35 Smoked Chicken

Light and fresh
Preparation time 15 minutes
Serves 4–6

675 g (1½ lb) smoked chicken

1½ tablespoons groundnut (peanut) oil

3 tablespoons chopped garlic

1 tablespoon coarsely chopped fresh root ginger

450 g (1 lb) (4 cups) Chinese leaves (Chinese cabbage), coarsely chopped

1 tablespoon dark soy sauce

1 tablespoon Shaoxing rice wine or dry sherry

Smoked chicken and duck are very popular in China. Such delicacies require a time-consuming smoking process that, fortunately, is done for us. They are readily available in supermarkets and Chinese grocers, thus making this northern Chinese favourite both appetising and easy to make. Serve with rice (see page 135) and a salad.

1 With your fingers, tear the meat from the bones of the chicken. Cut it into large shreds and set aside.

2 Heat a wok or large frying pan and add the groundnut oil, garlic and ginger. Stir-fry for 10 seconds, then add the Chinese leaves and stir-fry for 5 minutes.

3 Add the soy sauce and rice wine or dry sherry and cook for another minute. Then add the smoked chicken and heat through. Serve at once.

36 Chicken Livers with Onions

Informal supper
Preparation time 15 minutes
Serves 2–4

450 g (1 lb) chicken livers, cut into bite-sized pieces

5 teaspoons Shaoxing rice wine or dry sherry

1 tablespoon light soy sauce

½ teaspoon five-spice powder

1 teaspoon salt

¼ teaspoon freshly ground black pepper

1 tablespoon cornflour (cornstarch)

Chicken livers are among the easiest foods to prepare. The trick is to combine them with the proper seasonings and spices so that their delicacy is retained but they are also given a new dimension. Hence the onions and the five-spice powder in this recipe – and it works! Serve this dish as part of a Chinese meal or as a main course (entrée) with rice (see page 135) and a vegetable. Calves' liver may be substituted for the chicken livers if you wish.

1 Combine the chicken livers with 3 teaspoons of the rice wine or dry sherry, the soy sauce, five-spice powder, ½ teaspoon of the salt, the pepper and cornflour. Mix well.

2 Heat a wok or large frying pan, then add 2 teaspoons of the groundnut oil. Add the livers and stir-fry for about 4 minutes, until they are brown on the outside but still pink inside. Remove the livers from the wok.

(continued opposite)

5 teaspoons groundnut
(peanut) oil

2 onions, sliced

2 teaspoons sesame oil

3 Wipe the wok clean, then reheat. Add the remaining oil, the remaining salt and the onions. Stir-fry for 4 minutes or until the onions are brown and slightly caramelised. Return the livers to the wok and add the remaining 2 teaspoons of rice wine or sherry and the sesame oil. Stir-fry for 2 minutes, then serve at once.

37 Five-spice Chicken

Hot and spicy
Preparation time 25 minutes
Serves 2–4

450 g (1 lb) boneless, skinless chicken breasts

1 tablespoon groundnut
(peanut) oil

1 teaspoon salt

2 tablespoons finely chopped red chilli peppers

2 teaspoons five-spice powder

2 teaspoons sesame oil

3 tablespoons finely chopped spring onions (scallions)

freshly ground white pepper

FOR THE MARINADE:

2 teaspoons light soy sauce

1 teaspoon Shaoxing rice wine or dry sherry

1 teaspoon cornflour
(cornstarch)

Five spice is an exotic, ancient spice formula that harmonises star anise, Sichuan peppercorns, fennel, cloves and cinnamon or the stronger-scented cassia into a special culinary experience. It is excellent used in a quick stir-fry dish, as it can quickly infuse the ingredients with a pungent, fragrant, hot, mild and slightly sweet aroma. Its distinct fragrance and unique flavour make any dish a treat.

1 Cut the chicken breasts into 2.5 cm (1 inch) cubes. Combine them with the marinade ingredients in a small bowl and refrigerate for about 15 minutes.

2 Heat a wok or large frying pan until it is very hot and then add the oil. When the oil is very hot and slightly smoking, add the chicken, together with the salt, chilli peppers, five-spice powder and some white pepper. Stir-fry for 4 minutes or until the chicken is cooked.

3 Stir in the sesame oil, give the mixture a couple of turns and cook for 3 minutes. Finally add the spring onions and stir-fry for another minute. Turn on to a platter and serve at once.

38 Chicken with Chinese and Button Mushrooms

Easy entertaining
Preparation time 40 minutes
Serves 4

450 g (1 lb) boneless, skinless chicken thighs or 900 g (2 lb) chicken thighs on the bone

2 tablespoons Chinese dried mushrooms

350 g (12 oz) (1½ cups) button mushrooms

1½ tablespoons groundnut (peanut) oil

1 onion, thinly sliced

2 tablespoons coarsely chopped garlic

2 teaspoons salt

½ teaspoon freshly ground five-pepper mixture or black pepper

2 teaspoons finely grated orange zest

2 tablespoons Shaoxing rice wine or dry sherry

3 tablespoons oyster sauce

2 teaspoons sugar

a large handful of fresh basil leaves

FOR THE MARINADE:

2 teaspoons light soy sauce

2 teaspoons Shaoxing rice wine or dry sherry

1 teaspoon sesame oil

2 teaspoons cornflour (cornstarch)

Here I have combined chicken with two kinds of mushrooms, the dried black ones so popular in Chinese cooking and plain button mushrooms. The textures of the mushrooms are wonderfully chewy, which adds richness to this unusually tasty dish.

1 Remove the skin and bones from unboned chicken thighs or ask your butcher to do it for you. Cut the chicken into 2.5 cm (1 inch) chunks and combine them in a bowl with all the marinade ingredients. Leave to marinate for 20 minutes at room temperature.

2 Meanwhile, soak the Chinese mushrooms in warm water for 20 minutes. Drain them, squeeze out the excess liquid and discard all the water. Remove and discard the stems and cut the caps into thick strips. Slice the button mushrooms.

3 Heat a wok or large frying pan until it is very hot, add the groundnut oil and then the chicken. Stir-fry for 5 minutes, until the chicken is brown. Remove the chicken and drain off most of the oil, leaving just 2 teaspoons in the pan.

4 Reheat the pan until it is hot, quickly add the onion and garlic and stir-fry for 2 minutes. Then add the salt, pepper, Chinese mushrooms and button mushrooms and stir-fry for 1 minute.

5 Return the chicken to the pan, add the orange zest and rice wine or sherry and stir-fry for 4 minutes, until the liquid has evaporated. Finally, add the oyster sauce, sugar and basil leaves, give the mixture a good stir and cook for another minute. Serve at once.

39 Vietnamese-style Lemongrass Chicken

Light and fresh
Preparation time 80 minutes
Serves 4

450 g (1 lb) boneless, skinless chicken thighs or 900 g (2 lb) chicken thighs on the bone

1 tablespoon groundnut (peanut) oil

175 g (6 oz) (¾ cup) onions, thinly sliced

6 garlic cloves, crushed

1 tablespoon finely chopped fresh root ginger

2 red or green chilli peppers, deseeded and coarsely chopped

2 teaspoons sugar

100 g (4 oz) (1 cup) roasted peanuts, coarsely chopped

1 tablespoon fish sauce (*nam pla*)

FOR THE MARINADE:

5 fresh lemongrass stalks

1 teaspoon salt

½ teaspoon freshly ground black pepper

3 tablespoons finely chopped spring onions (scallions)

Lemongrass (*Cymbopogon citratus*) is a tropical grass native to southern India and Sri Lanka. It yields an aromatic oil used as a flavouring and in perfumery and medicine. It often appears in Vietnamese dishes, giving a wonderful citrus aroma. I especially like its use with chicken, and here is a Vietnamese-inspired recipe redolent with lemongrass. It is a tasty dish that is relatively easy to make. Instead of using a whole chicken, I use chicken thighs, which I find more flavoursome and easier to handle.

1 Remove the skin and bones from unboned chicken thighs or ask your butcher do it for you. Cut the chicken into 2.5 cm (1 inch) pieces.

2 Peel the lemongrass stalks to reveal the tender, whitish centre. Crush with the flat of a knife and cut into pieces 7.5 cm (3 inches) long.

3 In a large bowl, combine the chicken with all the marinade ingredients, including the lemongrass, and leave to marinate at room temperature for 45 minutes.

4 Heat a wok or large frying pan over a high heat, then add the oil. When it is very hot and slightly smoking, turn the heat to low, add the chicken, together with the marinade ingredients, and stir-fry for 5 minutes.

5 Add the onions, garlic, ginger and chillies and stir-fry for 10 minutes. Add the sugar and peanuts and stir-fry for 2 minutes. Finally, add the fish sauce and continue to stir-fry for 2 minutes, mixing all the ingredients well. Transfer to a warm platter and serve at once.

40 Indonesian-style Chicken with Vegetables

Informal supper
Preparation time 35 minutes
Serves 4–6

225 g (8 oz) (1 head) broccoli

225 g (8 oz) asparagus

225 g (8 oz) (1 cup) baby sweetcorn

3 tablespoons groundnut (peanut) oil

450 g (1 lb) boneless, skinless chicken thighs, cut into 2.5 cm (1 inch) pieces

2 tablespoons finely sliced garlic

3 tablespoons finely sliced shallots

2 large, fresh red chilli peppers, deseeded and sliced

1 tablespoon finely sliced fresh root ginger

1½ tablespoons light soy sauce

2 teaspoons shrimp paste

2 teaspoons sugar

1 teaspoon salt

225 g (8 oz) (1 cup) button mushrooms, thinly sliced

2 tablespoons Chicken Stock (see page 134) or water

freshly ground black pepper

This is a typically hearty, family-style stir-fry that I have encountered numerous times in Jakarta. Indonesian cooks do not marinate their meat in the Chinese manner, with soy sauce, rice wine, etc. However, they often stir-fry it with pungent, aromatic ingredients such as shrimp paste and chilli peppers. The results are just as tasty, and perfect for a large crowd.

1 Cut the stalks off the broccoli and divide the heads into small florets. Peel the stalks and thinly slice them on the diagonal. Trim the woody ends off the asparagus and then cut into 4 cm (1½ inch) lengths.

2 Blanch the broccoli and baby sweetcorn in a large pan of boiling salted water for 3 minutes. Drain, and plunge them into cold water to stop them cooking further, then drain again.

3 Heat a wok or large frying pan over a high heat. Add the oil and, when it is very hot and slightly smoking, add the chicken pieces and stir-fry for 5 minutes or until golden brown. Remove the chicken with a slotted spoon and leave to drain in a colander or sieve.

4 Reheat the wok over a high heat until it is medium hot. Add the garlic, shallots, chilli peppers and ginger and stir-fry for about 2 minutes, until golden brown. Then add the soy sauce, shrimp paste, sugar, salt and pepper and stir-fry for 1 minute.

5 Now add the broccoli, corn, asparagus and mushrooms and continue to stir-fry for 3 minutes.

6 Return the drained chicken to the wok, add the stock or water and cook over a high heat for 5 minutes or until the chicken is thoroughly cooked. Turn out on to a platter and serve at once.

41 Thai Green Curry Chicken with Aubergines

Easy entertaining
Preparation time 15 minutes
Serves 4

450 g (1 lb) boneless, skinless chicken thighs or 900 g (2 lb) chicken thighs on the bone

1 kg (2¼ lb) Chinese or ordinary aubergines (eggplant)

2 teaspoons light soy sauce

2 teaspoons Shaoxing rice wine or dry sherry

1 teaspoon sesame oil

2 teaspoons cornflour (cornstarch)

1½ tablespoons groundnut (peanut) oil

3 tablespoons chopped garlic

1 tablespoon finely chopped fresh root ginger

3 tablespoons finely chopped spring onions

2–3 tablespoons Thai green curry paste

1 tablespoon fish sauce (*nam pla*) or light soy sauce

2 teaspoons sugar

a large handful of fresh basil leaves

Thai dishes have become very popular in the West, especially with many chefs who are practising Fusion cuisine. No wonder – Thai cooking is full of enticingly fragrant aromas. Thai curry pastes can be time-consuming and laborious to make but fortunately there are now high-quality ones available in supermarkets. I find them perfectly acceptable and many have authentic Thai flavours.

This recipe is very popular and is often found in restaurants in Sydney. To cut down the fat, I roast the aubergines in the oven instead of frying them in the traditional Thai way, so they don't absorb any oil. This step can be done hours ahead and the rest is a quick stir-fry. Serve with plain steamed rice (see page 135).

1 Remove the skin and bones from unboned chicken thighs or ask your butcher to do it for you.

2 Preheat the oven to 200ºC/400ºF/Gas Mark 6 (fairly hot). Roast the aubergines until soft and cooked through – about 20 minutes for Chinese aubergines, 30–40 minutes for ordinary ones. Allow the aubergines to cool and then peel them. Put the flesh in a colander and leave to drain for at least 30 minutes. Chop the aubergine flesh.

3 Cut the chicken into 2.5 cm (1 inch) chunks and combine them in a bowl with the soy sauce, rice wine or sherry, sesame oil and cornflour.

4 Heat a wok or large frying pan until it is very hot, then add the groundnut oil, followed by the chicken. Stir-fry for 5 minutes, then remove the chicken and drain off most of the fat and oil, leaving 2 teaspoons in the wok.

5 Return the drained chicken to the wok, add the garlic, ginger and spring onions and stir-fry for 5 minutes. Then add the chopped aubergine flesh and all the remaining ingredients except the basil leaves. Cook for another 3 minutes, stirring from time to time. When the chicken is cooked, add the basil leaves and give the mixture a good stir. Transfer to a platter and serve at once.

42 Pineapple Chicken

Informal supper
Preparation time 40 minutes
Serves 4

450 g (1 lb) boneless, skinless chicken breasts

300 ml (10 fl oz) groundnut (peanut) oil or water

1 tablespoon groundnut (peanut) oil

1 tablespoon finely chopped fresh root ginger

1 tablespoon thinly sliced garlic

1½ tablespoons Shaoxing rice wine or dry sherry

1 teaspoon salt

1 teaspoon sesame oil

350 g (12 oz) (1½ cups) small pineapple, peeled, cored and cut into 2.5 cm (1 inch) pieces

1 tablespoon finely chopped fresh coriander (cilantro)

FOR THE MARINADE:

1 egg white

1 teaspoon sesame oil

2 teaspoons cornflour (cornstarch)

1 teaspoon salt

½ teaspoon white pepper

This might be called 'nouvelle Hong Kong' or 'South-east Asia meets Hong Kong'. It is an exotic and unlikely combination. I have eaten this dish several times in Hong Kong and found it delicious every time. The acidic sweetness and texture of the pineapple work extremely well with the delicate taste of the chicken. The pineapple is cooked very quickly, just enough to warm it through.

1 Cut the chicken into 2.5 cm (1 inch) pieces and place in a bowl. Add all the marinade ingredients, mix well and refrigerate for about 20 minutes.

2 If using groundnut oil to cook the chicken, heat a wok or frying pan over a high heat and then add the oil. When it is very hot, remove the wok from the heat and immediately add the chicken pieces, stirring vigorously to prevent them sticking. After about 2 minutes, when the chicken pieces turn white, quickly drain them in a stainless-steel colander set in a bowl. Discard the oil.

3 If you use water instead of oil, bring it to the boil in a saucepan, then remove from the heat and immediately add the chicken pieces, stirring vigorously to prevent them sticking. After about 2 minutes, when the chicken pieces turn white, quickly drain them in a colander set in a bowl. Discard the water.

4 If you used a wok or pan, wipe it clean. Reheat it over a high heat, then add the tablespoon of oil. Add the ginger and garlic and stir-fry for 30 seconds, then add the rice wine or dry sherry, salt, sesame oil and pineapple. Gently stir-fry for 2 minutes or until the pineapple is heated through.

5 Add the drained chicken and stir gently to mix well. Turn on to a warm platter, garnish with the coriander and serve at once.

43 Thai-style Duck

<table>
<tr><td>Easy entertaining</td></tr>
<tr><td>Preparation time 35 minutes</td></tr>
<tr><td>Serves 4</td></tr>
</table>

450 g (1 lb) boneless, skinless duck breasts

1 lemongrass stalk

3 tablespoons groundnut (peanut) oil

3 tablespoons finely sliced shallots

2 tablespoons coarsely chopped garlic

1 tablespoon fish sauce (*nam pla*) or light soy sauce

1 teaspoon dark soy sauce

2 teaspoons finely grated lime zest

3 large, fresh red or green chilli peppers, deseeded and finely shredded

2 teaspoons sugar

a large handful of fresh basil leaves

FOR THE MARINADE:

2 teaspoons light soy sauce

2 teaspoons Shaoxing rice wine or dry sherry

2 teaspoons sesame oil

¼ teaspoon salt

2 teaspoons cornflour (cornstarch)

freshly ground black pepper

I often think that duck is a neglected food and that everyone is terrified of cooking it. Fortuitously, duck breasts are now available in many supermarkets. They are perfect for a quick stir-fry and can add a new dimension to your cooking repertoire. The flesh has the advantage of being meaty and lean at the same time. Its rich flavour makes it an ideal partner for assertive Thai spices.

1 Cut the duck breasts into slices 4 cm (1½ inches) long and 1 cm (½ inch) thick. Put the duck slices into a bowl, add all the marinade ingredients and mix well. Let the slices steep in the marinade for about 15 minutes.

2 Peel the lemongrass stalk to reveal the tender, whitish centre and cut it into 5 cm (2 inch) pieces. Crush with the flat of a cleaver or knife and set aside.

3 Heat a wok or large frying pan over a high heat until it is very hot. Add the oil and, when it is very hot and slightly smoking, add the duck from the marinade and stir-fry for about 2 minutes; it should be slightly pink in the centre. Remove the duck and drain it in a colander.

4 Pour off all but 1½ tablespoons of the oil from the pan and reheat it over a high heat. Add the lemongrass, shallots and garlic and stir-fry for 3 minutes. Now add the fish sauce, dark soy sauce, lime zest, chilli peppers and sugar and stir-fry for 1 minute.

5 Return the drained duck to the wok or pan. Stir to mix well, toss in the basil leaves, give it a good stir and transfer to a platter. Serve at once.

44 Mango Prawns

Light and fresh
Preparation time 50 minutes
Serves 4

450 g (1 lb) raw prawns (green shrimp)

2 tablespoons salt

450 ml (15 fl oz) groundnut (peanut) oil or water

1½ tablespoons groundnut (peanut) oil

1½ tablespoons finely chopped fresh root ginger

2 teaspoons finely chopped garlic

1 tablespoon Shaoxing rice wine or dry sherry

1 teaspoon salt

½ teaspoon freshly ground white pepper

2 large mangoes, peeled, pitted and cut into cubes

2 teaspoons sesame oil

2 tablespoons finely chopped spring onions (scallions)

FOR THE MARINADE:

1 egg white

2 teaspoons cornflour (cornstarch)

1 teaspoon salt

1 teaspoon sesame oil

½ teaspoon freshly ground white pepper

This exotic and unlikely combination is one of the best examples of how Chinese food practices evolve in Hong Kong, with the new and the foreign being joined to the venerable and the native. The rich sweetness of the mango complements the fresh sea fragrance and delicate taste of the prawns.

1 Peel the prawns, make a slit down the back of each and pull out the fine digestive cord with the tip of the knife. Wash the prawns in cold water with a tablespoon of salt, then drain and repeat. Rinse well and pat dry with kitchen paper.

2 Combine the prawns with all the marinade ingredients, mix well and leave in the refrigerator for 20 minutes.

3 If using groundnut oil to cook the prawns, heat a wok or large frying pan over a high heat and then add the oil. When it is very hot, remove the wok or pan from the heat and immediately add the prawns, stirring vigorously to prevent them sticking. When they turn white, after about 2 minutes, quickly drain the prawns in a stainless-steel colander set in a bowl. Discard the oil.

4 If you use water instead of oil, bring it to the boil in a saucepan, then remove from the heat and immediately add the prawns, stirring vigorously to prevent them sticking. When the prawns turn white, after about 2 minutes, quickly drain them in a colander set in a bowl. Discard the water.

5 If you used a wok or pan, wipe it clean. Reheat it until it is very hot. Add the 1½ tablespoons of groundnut oil and, when it is very hot and slightly smoking, add the ginger and garlic and stir-fry for 10 seconds.

6 Return the prawns to the wok or pan, together with the rice wine or dry sherry, salt and pepper. Stir-fry the mixture for 1 minute.

7 Add the mango pieces and stir gently for 1 minute to warm them through, then stir in the sesame oil. Turn on to a warm serving platter, garnish with the spring onions and serve.

45 Hot and Sour Indonesian Prawns

Informal supper
Preparation time 25 minutes
Serves 4

450 g (1 lb) raw prawns (green shrimp)

2 tablespoons salt

1½ tablespoons groundnut (peanut) oil

1 small onion, chopped

1 tablespoon finely chopped garlic

2 teaspoons finely chopped fresh root ginger

2 fresh red chilli peppers, deseeded and chopped

1 teaspoon ground cumin

1 teaspoon ground coriander

1 teaspoon shrimp paste

1 teaspoon sugar

3 tablespoons lemon juice

Seafood is a staple of the Indonesian diet. This simple but delectable dish is typical of the cooking found in many homes. Prawns cook quickly, so they make ideal fast food. Serve with plain rice (see page 135) for a complete meal.

1 Peel the prawns, make a slit down the back of each one and pull out the fine digestive cord with the tip of the knife. Wash the prawns in cold water with a tablespoon of salt, then drain and repeat. Rinse well and pat dry with kitchen paper.

2 Heat a wok or large frying pan over a high heat. Add the oil and, when it is very hot and slightly smoking, add the onion, garlic, ginger and chilli peppers and stir-fry for 3 minutes.

3 Add the cumin, coriander and shrimp paste and stir-fry for 1 minute. Now add the sugar and prawns and stir-fry for 2 minutes.

4 Add the lemon juice, reduce the heat and simmer for 4 minutes or until most of the liquid has evaporated. Serve immediately.

46 Stir-fried *Persillade* Prawns

East meets West
Preparation time 60 minutes
Serves 4

450 g (1 lb) raw prawns (green shrimp)

2 tablespoons salt

450 ml (15 fl oz) groundnut (peanut) oil or water

1 tablespoon extra virgin olive oil

FOR THE MARINADE:

1 egg white

2 teaspoons cornflour (cornstarch)

1 teaspoon salt

1 teaspoon sesame oil

1/2 teaspoon freshly ground white pepper

FOR THE PERSILLADE:

2 tablespoons extra virgin olive oil

1 1/2 teaspoons finely chopped fresh root ginger

2 tablespoons finely chopped garlic

1/2 teaspoon sugar

1 tablespoon finely chopped spring onions (scallions)

1 tablespoon finely chopped fresh coriander (cilantro)

3 tablespoons finely chopped fresh parsley

salt and ground black pepper

Persillade is a French culinary term referring to a mixture of chopped parsley and garlic that is usually added to dishes at the end of the cooking process. This robust seasoning gives any dish a distinctly assertive flavour. In this recipe, I have added an Eastern touch of fresh coriander and ginger to the *persillade*, giving a refreshing new dimension to a classic seasoning. *Persillade* goes particularly well with a dish such as prawns. Serve drizzled with Garlic, Ginger and Spring Onion Oil (see page 136), if liked.

1 Peel the prawns, make a slit down the back of each one and pull out the fine digestive cord with the tip of the knife. Wash the prawns in cold water with a tablespoon of salt, then drain and repeat. Rinse well and pat dry with kitchen paper.

2 Combine the prawns with all the marinade ingredients, mix well and leave in the refrigerator for 20 minutes.

3 Combine all the *persillade* ingredients in a food processor or blender and process until finely chopped. If you are using a blender, be careful not to overblend the mixture to a purée.

4 If using groundnut oil to cook the prawns, heat a wok or large frying pan over a high heat and then add the oil. When it is very hot, remove the wok or pan from the heat and immediately add the prawns, stirring vigorously to prevent them sticking. When they turn white, after about 2 minutes, quickly drain the prawns in a stainless-steel colander set in a bowl. Discard the oil.

5 If you use water instead of oil, bring it to the boil in a saucepan, then remove from the heat and immediately add the prawns, stirring vigorously to prevent them sticking. When the prawns turn white, after about 2 minutes, quickly drain them in a colander set in a bowl. Discard the water.

6 If you used a wok or pan, wipe it clean. Reheat it until it is very hot, then add the olive oil. When it is hot, return the prawns to the wok and stir-fry for 20 seconds. Quickly stir in the *persillade* mixture and mix well. Turn on to a platter and serve at once.

47 Prawns with Egg

Informal supper
Preparation time 45 minutes
Serves 4

225 g (8 oz) raw prawns (green shrimp)

2 tablespoons salt

2 tablespoons groundnut (peanut) oil

3 tablespoons chopped spring onions (scallions), green part only

FOR THE MARINADE:

1 egg white

1 teaspoon salt

$\frac{1}{2}$ teaspoon freshly ground white pepper

1 teaspoon sesame oil

2 teaspoons cornflour (cornstarch)

FOR THE EGG MIXTURE:

6 large eggs, beaten

2 teaspoons sesame oil

3 tablespoons Chicken Stock (see page 134) or water

1 tablespoon Shaoxing rice wine or dry sherry

1 teaspoon salt

$\frac{1}{2}$ teaspoon freshly ground black pepper

1 tablespoon light soy sauce

1 teaspoon sugar

This dish is commonly known in the West as egg fuyung. It is popular because it is light and delicious, easy to make and uses familiar ingredients. I think it is at its best made with good-quality prawns but you could substitute crab, fish or even minced (ground) pork or beef, if you like.

1 Peel the prawns, make a slit down the back of each one and pull out the fine digestive cord with the tip of the knife. Wash the prawns in cold water with a tablespoon of salt, then drain and repeat. Rinse well and pat dry with kitchen paper.

2 Combine the prawns with all the marinade ingredients, mix well and leave in the refrigerator for 20 minutes.

3 Put all the ingredients for the egg mixture in a bowl and mix well, then set aside.

4 Heat a wok or large frying pan until it is very hot and add 1 tablespoon of the groundnut oil. When it is very hot and slightly smoking, add the prawns and stir-fry for 2 minutes. Remove with a slotted spoon.

5 Wipe the wok or pan clean, reheat it over a high heat, then add the remaining tablespoon of oil. Quickly add the egg mixture and stir-fry for 1 minute, until the eggs begin to set. Return the prawns to the wok and continue to stir-fry for 1 minute. Garnish with the spring onions and serve at once.

48 Sweet and Sour Prawns

Classic Chinese
Preparation time 35 minutes
Serves 4

450 g (1 lb) raw prawns
(green shrimp)

2 tablespoons salt

1½ tablespoons groundnut
(peanut) oil

1 tablespoon chopped garlic

2 teaspoons finely chopped
fresh root ginger

4 spring onions (scallions), cut
on the diagonal into 4 cm
(1½ inch) lengths

100 g (4 oz) (about 1) red or
green pepper (bell pepper), cut
into 2.5 cm (1 inch) dice

225 g (8 oz) (1 cup) water
chestnuts (peeled if fresh,
rinsed if canned), sliced

FOR THE SAUCE:

150 ml (5 fl oz) Chicken Stock
(see page 134)

2 tablespoons Shaoxing rice
wine or dry sherry

3 tablespoons light soy sauce

2 teaspoons dark soy sauce

1½ tablespoons tomato purée

3 tablespoons Chinese white
rice vinegar or cider vinegar

1 tablespoon sugar

1 tablespoon cornflour
(cornstarch), blended with 2
tablespoons water

This is a very popular Chinese dish in the West. The sweet and pungent flavours of the sauce combine well with the firm, succulent prawns. It is simple to make and can be served as part of a Chinese meal or on its own as a starter for a European meal.

1 Peel the prawns, make a slit down the back of each one and pull out the fine digestive cord with the tip of the knife. Wash the prawns in cold water with a tablespoon of salt, then drain and repeat. Rinse well and pat dry with kitchen paper.

2 Heat a wok or large frying pan until it is very hot. Add the oil, and when it is very hot and slightly smoking, add the garlic, ginger and spring onions and stir-fry for 20 seconds. Then add the prawns and stir-fry for 10 seconds. Add the pepper and water chestnuts and stir-fry for a further 30 seconds.

3 Add all the sauce ingredients, bring to the boil, then turn down the heat and simmer for 4 minutes. Serve immediately, with plain steamed rice (see page 135).

49 Prawn and Pork Stir-fry

Easy entertaining
Preparation time 55 minutes
Serves 4

225 g (8 oz) raw prawns (green shrimp)

2 tablespoons salt

450 ml (15 fl oz) groundnut (peanut) oil or water

1 tablespoon groundnut (peanut) oil

2 tablespoons coarsely chopped salted black beans

1½ tablespoons finely chopped fresh root ginger

2 teaspoons finely chopped garlic

450 g (1 lb) minced (ground) pork

1 tablespoon dark soy sauce

2 teaspoons light soy sauce

1 tablespoon Shaoxing rice wine or dry sherry

½ teaspoon sugar

2 teaspoons sesame oil

2 tablespoons finely chopped spring onions (scallions)

salt and freshly ground white pepper

FOR THE MARINADE:

1 egg white

2 teaspoons cornflour (cornstarch)

1 teaspoon sesame oil

salt and ground white pepper

The Chinese combine foods in an unusual way, sometimes mixing seafood with meats, especially pork. The result is delicious, savoury and very tasty. Here minced pork is used to extend the more expensive prawns. This recipe is equally good made with fresh scallops.

1 Peel the prawns, make a slit down the back of each one and pull out the fine digestive cord with the tip of the knife. Wash the prawns in cold water with a tablespoon of salt, then drain and repeat. Rinse well and pat dry with kitchen paper.

2 Combine the prawns with all the marinade ingredients, mix well and leave in the refrigerator for 20 minutes.

3 If using groundnut oil to cook the prawns, heat a wok or large frying pan over a high heat and then add the oil. When it is very hot, remove the wok or pan from the heat and immediately add the prawns, stirring vigorously to prevent them sticking. When they turn white, after about 2 minutes, quickly drain the prawns in a stainless-steel colander set in a bowl. Discard the oil.

4 If you use water instead of oil, bring it to the boil in a saucepan, then remove from the heat and immediately add the prawns, stirring vigorously to prevent them sticking. When the prawns turn white, after about 2 minutes, quickly drain them in a colander set in a bowl. Discard the water.

5 If you used a wok or pan, wipe it clean. Reheat it until it is very hot, add the tablespoon of oil and, when it is very hot and slightly smoking, add the black beans, ginger and garlic and stir-fry for 10 seconds.

6 Add the pork and continue to stir-fry for 5 minutes. Drain the pork of any excess oil and return it to the wok.

7 Add the prawns to the wok, together with the soy sauces, rice wine or dry sherry, salt, pepper and sugar. Stir-fry the mixture for 1 minute, then stir in the sesame oil. Turn on to a warm platter, garnish with the spring onions and serve at once.

50 Hot Pepper Prawns

Hot and spicy
Preparation time 20 minutes
Serves 4

450 g (1 lb) raw prawns
(green shrimp)

2 tablespoons salt, plus
1 teaspoon salt

2 teaspoons cornflour
(cornstarch)

2 teaspoons sesame oil

2 tablespoons groundnut
(peanut) oil

2 fresh chilli peppers, deseeded
and coarsely chopped

1 tablespoon salted black beans

2 tablespoons coarsely
chopped garlic

4 tablespoons coarsely
chopped spring onions
(scallions)

3 tablespoons white rice vinegar

2 tablespoons dark soy sauce

1 tablespoon sugar

2 teaspoons cornflour
(cornstarch), blended with 2
teaspoons water

I was introduced to this dish one evening when I dined with Madhur Jaffrey and her husband at the Shun Lee Palace restaurant in New York. She suggested that I try it, predicting that I would appreciate the imaginative interplay of pungent aromas and spicy flavours. How right she was. This is an exciting treat for the taste buds and very easy to prepare. Serve it with rice (see page 135). For a one-dish meal, double the quantity of sauce and toss the sauce and prawns with fresh egg noodles or rice noodles.

1 Peel the prawns, make a slit down the back of each one and pull out the fine digestive cord with the tip of the knife. Wash the prawns in cold water with a tablespoon of salt, then drain and repeat. Rinse well and pat dry with kitchen paper.

2 Combine with the teaspoon of salt, plus the cornflour and sesame oil and mix well.

3 Heat a wok or large frying pan and add the groundnut oil and prawns. Stir-fry for 1 minute, then remove the prawns with a slotted spoon. Add the chilli peppers, black beans, garlic and spring onions to the wok and stir-fry for 20 seconds.

4 Add the vinegar, soy sauce and sugar. Stir in the cornflour mixture and return the prawns to the wok. Cook for another 2 minutes, then serve at once.

51 Prawns and Scallops in Black Bean and Tomato Butter Sauce

East meets West
Preparation time 35 minutes
Serves 4

450 g (1 lb) raw prawns (green shrimp)

2 tablespoons salt

1½ tablespoons olive oil

450 g (1 lb) fresh scallops, including the corals

1½ tablespoons coarsely chopped garlic

1 tablespoon finely chopped fresh root ginger

2 tablespoons finely chopped shallots

1 tablespoon coarsely chopped salted black beans

1 tablespoon Shaoxing rice wine or dry sherry

1 tablespoon light soy sauce

120 ml (4 fl oz) Fish Stock or Chicken Stock (see page 134)

175 g (6 oz) (1 cup) tomatoes, skinned and deseeded if fresh, drained if tinned, then coarsely chopped

25 g (1 oz) (2 tablespoons) cold unsalted butter, cut into small pieces

a small handful of fresh basil leaves, cut into strips, to garnish

It doesn't surprise me to see Fusion cooks all over the world using Chinese black beans. Their distinctive, salty, pungent taste imparts a rich flavour to the foods they are cooked with. Now widely available, these black beans transform ordinary dishes into a special treat. In this recipe, prawns and scallops are stir-fried with the black beans and then finished off with a European touch in the form of a tomato butter sauce. It makes an elegant dinner-party main course, served with vegetables. Drizzle with Chive-flavoured Olive Oil (see page 136).

1 Peel the prawns, make a slit down the back of each one and pull out the fine digestive cord with the tip of the knife. Wash the prawns in cold water with a table-spoon of the salt, then drain and repeat. Rinse well and pat dry with kitchen paper.

2 Heat a wok or large frying pan over a high heat. Add the olive oil, then the prawns and scallops, and stir-fry for 2 minutes. Remove the prawns and scallops with a slotted spoon and set aside.

3 Add the garlic, ginger and shallots and stir-fry for 30 seconds. Then add the black beans and stir-fry for another 30 seconds. Add the rice wine or sherry, light soy sauce and stock, cover and cook over a high heat for 1 minute.

4 Return the scallops and prawns to the wok or pan and cook for 3 minutes, until just tender. Finally, add the chopped tomatoes and, when the mixture is hot, slowly whisk in the butter a piece at a time. Turn on to a warm serving platter, garnish with the basil and serve at once.

52 Prawns in Ginger Sauce

Easy entertaining
Preparation time 20 minutes
Serves 4

450 g (1 lb) raw prawns
(green shrimp)

2 tablespoons salt, plus
1 teaspoon salt

1 teaspoon cornflour
(cornstarch)

1 teaspoon sesame oil

1½ tablespoons groundnut
(peanut) oil

3 tablespoons finely chopped
fresh root ginger

FOR THE SAUCE:

2 tablespoons Shaoxing rice
wine or dry sherry

1 tablespoon light soy sauce

1 tablespoon water

½ teaspoon salt

1 teaspoon sugar

2 tablespoons finely chopped
fresh coriander (cilantro)

2 teaspoons sesame oil

Again, one of my quick and easy favourites – this time prawns with a zesty ginger sauce to make a spicy and refreshing treat. This delightful and visually attractive recipe can be served over rice for a one-dish meal that will satisfy both the stomach and the palate. It can also double as a starter for a dinner party.

1 Peel the prawns, make a slit down the back of each one and pull out the fine digestive cord with the tip of the knife. Wash the prawns in cold water with a tablespoon of salt, then drain and repeat. Rinse well and pat dry with kitchen paper.

2 Combine the prawns with the teaspoon of salt, plus the cornflour and sesame oil. Heat a wok or large frying pan, then add the groundnut oil, followed by the prawns and ginger. Stir-fry the mixture for 30 seconds.

3 Add all the sauce ingredients and continue to cook for 2 minutes. Serve at once.

53 Prawns with Water Chestnuts

Classic Chinese
Preparation time 50 minutes
Serves 4

450 g (1 lb) raw prawns (green shrimp)

2 tablespoons salt, plus 1 teaspoon salt

225 g (8 oz) (1 cup) fresh or canned (drained weight) water chestnuts

175 g (6 oz) (1 cup) frozen small garden peas or petits pois

450 ml (15 fl oz) groundnut (peanut) oil or water

1 tablespoon groundnut (peanut) oil

1½ tablespoons finely chopped fresh root ginger

1 tablespoon chopped garlic

½ small onion, thinly sliced

1 tablespoon Shaoxing rice wine or dry sherry

½ teaspoon sugar

2 teaspoons sesame oil

2 tablespoons finely chopped spring onions (scallions)

freshly ground white pepper

FOR THE MARINADE:

1 egg white

1 teaspoon sesame oil

2 teaspoons cornflour (cornstarch)

salt and ground white pepper

This was a favourite with customers in the restaurant where I worked when I was young. It is easy to see why. Rich, tasty prawns are paired with crisp water chestnuts and sweet green peas. Light and delectable, it really is a most appealing dish.

1 Peel the prawns, make a slit down the back of each one and pull out the fine digestive cord with the tip of the knife. Wash the prawns in cold water with a tablespoon of salt, then drain and repeat. Rinse well and pat dry with kitchen paper.

2 Combine the prawns with all the marinade ingredients, mix well and leave in the refrigerator for 20 minutes.

3 Peel the water chestnuts if fresh, or rinse if canned, and slice. Put the peas in a small bowl and let them thaw.

4 If using groundnut oil to cook the prawns, heat a wok or large frying pan over a high heat and then add the oil. When it is very hot, remove the wok or pan from the heat and immediately add the prawns, stirring vigorously to prevent them sticking. When they turn white, after about 2 minutes, quickly drain the prawns in a stainless-steel colander set in a bowl. Discard the oil.

5 If you use water instead of oil, bring it to the boil in a saucepan, then remove from the heat and immediately add the prawns, stirring vigorously to prevent them sticking. When the prawns turn white, after about 2 minutes, quickly drain them in a colander set in a bowl. Discard the water.

6 If you used a wok or pan, wipe it clean. Reheat it until it is very hot and add the tablespoon of groundnut oil. When it is very hot and slightly smoking, add the ginger and garlic and stir-fry for 10 seconds. Add the onion and continue to stir-fry for 2 minutes.

7 Return the prawns to the wok, together with the water chestnuts, peas, rice wine or dry sherry, pepper, sugar and the teaspoon of salt. Stir-fry the mixture for 3 minutes, then stir in the sesame oil. Turn on to a platter, garnish with the spring onions and serve at once.

54 Sichuan-style Scallops

Hot and spicy
Preparation time 10 minutes
Serves 4

1½ tablespoons groundnut
(peanut) oil

1 tablespoon finely chopped
fresh root ginger

1 tablespoon finely chopped garlic

2 tablespoons finely chopped
spring onions (scallions)

450 g (1 lb) fresh scallops,
including the corals

FOR THE SAUCE:

1 tablespoon Shaoxing rice wine
or dry sherry

2 teaspoons light soy sauce

2 teaspoons dark soy sauce

2 tablespoons chilli bean sauce

2 teaspoons tomato purée

1 teaspoon sugar

½ teaspoon salt

½ teaspoon freshly ground white
pepper

2 teaspoons sesame oil

Scallops are a favourite with the Chinese, and stir-frying works especially well because if they are overcooked they become tough. Here they have a spicy Sichuan sauce, which goes well with plain rice (see page 135).

1 Heat a wok or large frying pan until it is very hot and add the oil. When it is very hot and slightly smoking, add the ginger, garlic and spring onions and stir-fry for 10 seconds. Add the scallops and stir-fry for 1 minute.

2 Add all the sauce ingredients except the sesame oil and stir-fry for 4 minutes, until the scallops are firm and thoroughly coated with the sauce.

3 Add the sesame oil and stir-fry for a minute longer. Serve at once.

55 Garlic Scallops

Easy entertaining
Preparation time 10 minutes
Serves 4

2 tablespoons groundnut (peanut) oil

6 tablespoons coarsely chopped garlic

450 g (1 lb) fresh scallops, including the corals

2 teaspoons finely shredded fresh root ginger

2 tablespoons deseeded and finely shredded fresh red chilli peppers

1 teaspoon salt

freshly ground white or black pepper

2 tablespoons finely chopped spring onions (scallions)

This is my adaptation of a wonderful scallop dish I enjoyed in a fishing village not far from Hong Kong. The scallops are quickly stir-fried in the wok, then showered with fried garlic and chilli peppers. The combination is unbeatable.

1 Heat a wok or large frying pan over a high heat. Add the oil, turn the heat to low and add the garlic. Allow it to fry gently until golden brown, then remove with a slotted spoon and drain on kitchen paper.

2 Reheat the oil and, when it is very hot and slightly smoking, add the scallops. Stir-fry for 30 seconds, until lightly browned. Immediately add the ginger and chilli peppers and stir-fry for 1 minute.

3 Add the salt and some pepper to taste. Stir-fry for 2 minutes, then stir in the fried garlic and spring onions, mix well and serve at once.

56 Spicy Scallops with Sun-dried Tomatoes

East meets West
Preparation time 10 minutes
Serves 4

1 tablespoon olive oil

2 teaspoons groundnut (peanut) oil

450 g (1 lb) fresh scallops, including the corals

2 teaspoons finely chopped fresh root ginger

2 tablespoons deseeded and finely shredded red chilli peppers

3 tablespoons finely chopped sun-dried tomatoes

2 teaspoons finely grated lemon zest

1 teaspoon sugar

2 tablespoons finely chopped fresh coriander (cilantro)

salt and freshly ground white or black pepper

Nothing is easier to stir-fry than fresh scallops, especially in a hot wok. The heat seals in all the goodness and juices. Here I have paired them with an unusual combination of sun-dried tomatoes, lemon and coriander for a light, refreshing flavour.

1 Heat a wok or large frying pan over a high heat and add the olive and groundnut oils. When they are very hot and slightly smoking, add the scallops and stir-fry for 30 seconds, until lightly browned.

2 Immediately add the ginger and chilli peppers and stir-fry for 1 minute. Then add the sun-dried tomatoes, lemon zest, sugar and some salt and pepper and stir-fry for 2 minutes.

3 Stir in the fresh coriander, mix well and serve at once.

57 Green Thai Curry Mussels

Easy entertaining
Preparation time 15 minutes
Serves 4–6

1.4 kg (3 lb) fresh mussels

450 ml (15 fl oz) canned coconut milk

1 tablespoon grated lime zest

1 tablespoon green Thai curry paste (or to taste)

3 tablespoons chopped fresh coriander (cilantro)

2 tablespoons fish sauce (*nam pla*)

1 teaspoon sugar

a large handful of fresh basil leaves

Whenever I have an unexpected crowd of friends for dinner, I naturally turn to mussels. They are easy to obtain, inexpensive and everyone has a good time eating them. Thai flavours have become so fashionable in recent years that a wide choice of green Thai curry pastes can now be found in supermarkets. Their popularity makes it easy to throw together a quick dinner. This simple dish (pictured opposite) can easily be increased for larger gatherings.

1 Scrub the mussels under cold running water, discarding any open ones that don't close when tapped lightly.

2 Pour the coconut milk into a wok or large frying pan. Add the lime zest, curry paste, coriander, fish sauce and sugar and bring to a simmer.

3 Add the mussels, then cover and cook for 5 minutes or until all the mussels have opened. Discard any that have difficulty opening. Give the mixture a final stir, add the basil leaves and serve at once.

58 Mussels in Black Bean Sauce

Informal supper
Preparation time 20 minutes
Serves 4–6

1.4 kg (3 lb) fresh mussels

2 tablespoons groundnut (peanut) oil

4 tablespoons coarsely chopped salted black beans

Mussels are an ideal 'quick and easy' food. Once they have been scrubbed clean in cold water to remove all sand, they cook very rapidly, announcing that they are done by cordially opening their shells. Make sure that they are all firmly closed before cooking – throw away any that do not close up when touched or that have damaged shells.

1 Scrub the mussels under cold running water, discarding any open ones that don't close when tapped lightly.

(continued overleaf)

3 tablespoons coarsely chopped garlic

2 tablespoons coarsely chopped fresh root ginger

2 tablespoons coarsely chopped spring onions (scallions)

2 teaspoons light soy sauce

2 Heat a wok or large frying pan and add the groundnut oil, black beans, garlic and ginger. Stir-fry for 20 seconds and add the mussels. Continue to cook for 5 minutes or until all the mussels have opened. Discard any that have difficulty opening or do not open at all.

3 Add the spring onions and soy sauce. Give the mixture a final stir and serve at once.

59 Spicy Salmon

Hot and spicy
Preparation time 10 minutes
Serves 4

4 thick-cut boneless salmon fillets, weighing about 100 g (4 oz) each, skinned

3 tablespoons groundnut (peanut) oil

3 tablespoons finely chopped spring onions (scallions)

FOR THE SPICE MIX:

1 teaspoon salt

1 teaspoon freshly ground black pepper

2 teaspoons chilli powder

1 teaspoon five-spice powder

1/2 teaspoon ground cumin

1/2 teaspoon ground coriander

1 teaspoon sugar

Fresh salmon is a quick fish to cook. Its rich, fatty flesh makes it an ideal foil for spices. Of course, it is important to get the highest-quality salmon you can afford, organic if possible. Lightly pan-fried in a hot wok, it makes a fast and wholesome meal.

1 Lay the salmon fillets on a platter. Put all the spices in a small bowl and mix well. Sprinkle the spice mixture evenly on both sides of the salmon fillets.

2 Heat a wok or frying pan over a high heat and add the oil. When the oil is slightly smoking, add the salmon fillets and sear on one side for 3–4 minutes. Turn over and sear the other side for another 3-4 minutes.

3 Transfer the salmon to a warm platter. Garnish with the spring onions and serve at once.

60 Squid with Chilli Peppers and Basil

Hot and spicy	
Preparation time 30 minutes	
Serves 4	

675 g (1½ lb) fresh squid (or 450 g/1 lb cleaned frozen squid, thawed)

175 g (6 oz) (1 cup) fresh or frozen petits pois

1½ tablespoons groundnut (peanut) oil

4 tablespoons coarsely chopped garlic

3 tablespoons finely sliced shallots

2–3 small, fresh red Thai chilli peppers, deseeded and chopped

1 tablespoon fish sauce (nam pla)

2 tablespoons oyster sauce

2 teaspoons sugar

a handful of fresh Thai basil leaves or ordinary basil leaves

Thai chefs are masters with seafood, especially squid. This aromatic stir-fried dish, known as *pla muk phat bai krapao*, is one of the simplest to cook and is flavoured with chilli peppers, basil and garlic – a mixture that is the essence of Thai cooking. Once the squid has been prepared, the dish takes very little time to complete. For maximum impact, delay the final cooking until the last possible moment.

1 Pull the head and tentacles of the squid away from the body; the intestines should come away with them. Then pull off the thin, purplish skin. Using a small, sharp knife, slit the body open; remove and discard the transparent bony section. Wash the body thoroughly under cold running water and cut it into 4 cm (1½ inch) strips.

2 Slice the tentacles off the head, cutting just above the eye (you may also have to remove the polyp, or beak, from the centre of the ring of tentacles). Discard the head and reserve the tentacles.

3 If you are using fresh peas, blanch them for 3 minutes in boiling salted water, then drain and set aside. If you are using frozen peas, simply thaw them and set them aside.

4 Heat a wok or large frying pan over a high heat and add the oil. When it is very hot and slightly smoking, add the garlic and stir-fry for 1 minute, until lightly browned. Remove with a slotted spoon and drain on kitchen paper.

5 Add the squid strips and tentacles to the wok and stir-fry for 1 minute, until beginning to turn opaque.

6 Add the shallots, chilli peppers, peas, fish sauce, oyster sauce and sugar and stir-fry for 3 minutes. Toss in the basil and give one last stir. Turn the mixture on to a platter, garnish with the fried garlic and serve at once.

61 Salmon with Lemon

Light and fresh
Preparation time 15 minutes
Serves 4

450 g (1 lb) boneless salmon fillet, skinned

2 teaspoons salt

4 tablespoons groundnut (peanut) oil

1 tablespoon finely shredded fresh root ginger

1 teaspoon sugar

1 tablespoon finely grated lemon zest

1 lemon, peeled and segmented

2 teaspoons sesame oil

salt and freshly ground black pepper

Once in Hong Kong, I enjoyed a salmon dish stir-fried with dried citrus peel. The tartness of the peel balanced the rich salmon nicely. I have adapted the idea by using fresh lemon, which works just as well. Fish should always be stir-fried gently, so as not to break up the delicate flesh.

1 Cut the salmon into strips 2.5 cm (1 inch) wide and sprinkle the salt evenly over them. Set aside for 20 minutes.

2 Heat a wok or large frying pan over a high heat and add 3 tablespoons of the groundnut oil. When it is very hot and slightly smoking, turn the heat down to medium and add the salmon strips. Let them fry undisturbed for about 2 minutes, until browned, then gently turn them over to brown the other side. Take care not to break them up. Remove with a slotted spoon and drain on kitchen paper. Wipe the wok clean.

3 Reheat the wok and add the remaining oil. Then add the ginger and stir-fry for 20 seconds to brown. Now add the sugar, lemon zest, lemon segments and some salt and pepper and stir-fry gently for about 1 minute.

4 Return the salmon to the wok and gently mix with the lemon for about 1 minute. Add the sesame oil and give the mixture a good stir. Using a slotted spoon, arrange the salmon and lemon on a warm serving platter and serve at once.

62 Fish with Black Bean Sauce

Classic Chinese
Preparation time 15 minutes
Serves 4

450 g (1 lb) fresh, firm white fish fillets, such as cod, halibut or sea bass, skinned

2 teaspoons salt

3 tablespoons groundnut (peanut) oil

1½ tablespoons coarsely chopped salted black beans

1 tablespoon finely chopped garlic

2 teaspoons finely chopped fresh root ginger

3 tablespoons finely chopped spring onions (scallions)

1 tablespoon light soy sauce

1 teaspoon dark soy sauce

1 tablespoon Shaoxing rice wine or dry sherry

1 teaspoon sugar

1 tablespoon water

2 teaspoons sesame oil

TO GARNISH:

3 tablespoons finely shredded spring onions (scallions)

My mother loved making this dish because it was quick, easy and delicious. The pungency of black beans, garlic and ginger turns ordinary fish into a gourmet's delight. When served with vegetables and rice, it becomes the type of light, wholesome, satisfying meal that is the hallmark of the best Chinese home cooking.

1 Cut the fish fillets into strips 2.5 cm (1 inch) wide and sprinkle the salt evenly over them. Set aside for 20 minutes.

2 Heat a wok or large frying pan over a high heat, then add the groundnut oil. When it is very hot and slightly smoking, turn the heat down to medium and add the fish strips. Stir-fry gently for about 2 minutes or until they are brown on both sides, taking care not to break them up. Remove them with a slotted spoon and drain on kitchen paper. Drain off all but 1½ tablespoons of the oil from the wok.

3 Re-heat the wok, then add the black beans, garlic, ginger and spring onions and stir-fry for 30 seconds. Add the soy sauces, rice wine or dry sherry, sugar and water and bring to a simmer.

4 Return the fish to the wok and gently finish cooking in the sauce for about 1 minute. Then add the sesame oil and give the mixture a good stir. Using a slotted spoon, arrange the fish on a warm serving platter, pour over the sauce, garnish with the spring onions and serve at once.

63 Fish with Peas

Informal supper
Preparation time 15 minutes
Serves 4

450 g (1 lb) fresh, firm white fish fillets, such as cod, halibut or sea bass, skinned

2 teaspoons salt

100 g (4 oz) (½ cup) fresh or frozen peas

2 tablespoons groundnut (peanut) oil

4 slices Parma ham or 2–3 slices lean smoked bacon, shredded

FOR THE SAUCE:

150 ml (5 fl oz) Chicken Stock (see page 134)

1 tablespoon Shaoxing rice wine or dry sherry

1 tablespoon light soy sauce

1 teaspoon salt

½ teaspoon freshly ground white pepper

2 teaspoons sugar

2 teaspoons cornflour (cornstarch), blended with 2 teaspoons water

2 teaspoons sesame oil

This dish is a favourite in southern China, especially when made with grouper, a firm, white, fleshy fish. However, it works equally well with cod fillets. It is important to use a firm-textured fish that will not fall apart during the stir-frying process.

1 Cut the fish fillets into strips 2.5 cm (1 inch) wide and sprinkle the salt evenly over them. Set aside for 20 minutes.

2 If you are using fresh peas, cook them for 5 minutes in a pan of boiling water and then drain in a colander. If you are using frozen peas, simply thaw them.

3 Heat a wok or large frying pan until it is very hot, then add the groundnut oil. When it is very hot and slightly smoking, add the fish strips. Stir-fry gently for about 2 minutes, taking care not to break them up.

4 Add the Parma ham or bacon, peas, stock, rice wine or dry sherry, soy sauce, salt, pepper and sugar. Bring the sauce to the boil, then add the cornflour mixture and stir this in well. Cook for another minute, stir in the sesame oil and serve at once.

64 Quick Beancurd in Spicy Chilli Sauce

Hot and spicy
Preparation time 15 minutes
Serves 4–6

450 g (1 lb) (2 cups) firm, fresh beancurd (tofu)

1 tablespoon groundnut (peanut) oil

1 tablespoon coarsely chopped garlic

2 teaspoons finely chopped fresh root ginger

3 tablespoons chopped spring onions (scallions)

1 tablespoon whole yellow bean sauce

1 tablespoon tomato paste

2 teaspoons chilli bean sauce

2 teaspoons dark soy sauce

2 teaspoons sugar

2 teaspoons sesame oil

Solid beancurd is best for stir-frying; however, be careful not to stir too vigorously or it will crumble. Any leftovers can be added to some stock to make a quick soup.

1 Cut the beancurd into 1 cm (½ inch) cubes and leave to drain on kitchen paper for 20 minutes.

2 Heat a wok or large frying pan, then add the groundnut oil, garlic, ginger and spring onions and stir-fry for 30 seconds.

3 Add all the remaining ingredients except the beancurd and simmer for 5 minutes.

4 Add the beancurd to the sauce, simmer for 3 minutes, then serve.

65 Spicy Courgettes

Hot and spicy
Preparation time 10 minutes
Serves 4–6

2 tablespoons groundnut (peanut) oil

3 tablespoons coarsely chopped garlic

Courgettes lend themselves to stir-frying in the wok, especially with spices. This dish is not only healthy but will easily satisfy anyone with a craving for a tasty vegetarian meal. It also makes a lovely accompaniment to a main course (entrée).

1 Heat a wok or large frying pan and add the groundnut oil. When it is hot, add the garlic and stir-fry for 30 seconds. Then add the courgettes and stir-fry for 2 minutes.

(continued opposite)

675 g (1½ lb) (4 medium) courgettes (zucchini), cut into 2.5 cm (1 inch) cubes

2 tablespoons chilli bean sauce

1 tablespoon dark soy sauce

2 teaspoons light soy sauce

1 tablespoon Shaoxing rice wine or dry sherry

3 tablespoons water

2 teaspoons sesame oil

salt and freshly ground black pepper

2 Add the chilli bean sauce, soy sauces, rice wine or sherry, water and some salt and pepper. Cover and cook for 3–5 minutes, until the courgettes are tender. If the wok is dry, add another tablespoon of water.

3 When the courgettes are tender, stir in the sesame oil and serve at once.

66 Eggs and Corn with Spring Onions and Ginger

Informal supper
Preparation time 15 minutes
Serves 4

450 g (1 lb) corn on the cob or 275 g (10 oz) (1¼ cups) frozen sweetcorn

1 tablespoon groundnut (peanut) oil

3 tablespoons coarsely chopped spring onions (scallions)

2 teaspoons finely chopped fresh root ginger

1 teaspoon salt

4 eggs, lightly beaten

I often make this dish when I am hungry and need a sustaining, nutritious meal in a hurry. Corn has made its way from the West to China, and in Hong Kong especially you will find it a popular food. You can substitute fresh or frozen peas for the corn, if you wish.

1 If you are using fresh corn on the cob, clean it and remove the kernels with a sharp knife or cleaver – you should end up with about 275 g (10 oz) (1¼ cups). If you are using frozen corn, place it in a bowl and let it thaw at room temperature.

2 Heat a wok or large frying pan over a high heat and add the oil. Add the spring onions, ginger and salt and stir-fry for 10 seconds.

3 Add the corn and stir-fry for 2 minutes. Finally, turn the heat to medium, add the eggs and continue to cook for 2 minutes. Serve at once.

67 Asparagus in Black Bean Sauce

Easy entertaining
Preparation time 10 minutes
Serves 2

1 tablespoon groundnut (peanut) oil

2 teaspoons finely chopped fresh root ginger

2 teaspoons finely chopped garlic

2 tablespoons coarsely chopped salted black beans

2 teaspoons chilli bean sauce

450 g (1 lb) fresh asparagus, cut on the diagonal into 7.5 cm (3 inch) lengths

150 ml (5 fl oz) vegetable stock

1 teaspoon sugar

3 tablespoons Shaoxing rice wine or dry sherry

1 teaspoon sesame oil

Asparagus is such an exquisite treat that when it is in season it is worth buying as often as you can. Although it is not a traditional ingredient of south-east Asian cooking, it has been very quickly incorporated during the last few decades. It goes well with this pungent and robust black bean sauce, a traditional Chinese seasoning. This vegetarian dish can rival any expensive meat dish. With rice and perhaps one other light dish, it will make a meal for two.

1 Heat a wok or large frying pan and add the groundnut oil. When it is hot, add the ginger, garlic and black beans and stir-fry for a few seconds.

2 Add the chilli bean sauce and, a few seconds later, the asparagus and stir-fry for 2 minutes.

3 Stir in the stock, sugar and rice wine or sherry. Cook the mixture over a high heat for about 2 minutes, stirring continuously. Add the sesame oil, give the mixture a couple of stirs and serve at once.

68 Hot and Spicy Stir-fried Cabbage

Hot and spicy
Preparation time 10 minutes
Serves 4–6

450 g (1 lb) (about 4½ cups) cabbage, cut into strips about 1 cm (½ inch) wide

1½ tablespoons groundnut (peanut) oil

2 tablespoons coarsely chopped garlic

1 tablespoon coarsely chopped fresh root ginger

1 tablespoon dark soy sauce

1 tablespoon oyster sauce

2 teaspoons chilli bean sauce

2 teaspoons sesame oil

Cabbage has a distinctive but delicate flavour that adapts well to a wide range of seasonings. Because it is a 'cold' vegetable, I believe it needs the assistance or enhancement of something like zesty Sichuan spices, as in this recipe. This dish makes a delicious accompaniment to all types of main course (entrée). With rice and another quick vegetable dish, it may also serve as part of a vegetarian meal. You can use Chinese leaves (Chinese cabbage) instead of cabbage, if you wish.

1 Bring a large pan of salted water to the boil, add the cabbage and blanch for 2 minutes – this removes any harshness of flavour and brings out the sweet taste. Drain thoroughly.

2 Heat a wok or large frying pan, then add the oil, garlic and ginger and stir-fry for about 10 seconds.

3 Add the cabbage and stir-fry for 2 minutes. Add the sauces and sesame oil and cook for another 2 minutes. Serve at once.

69 Cauliflower with Fresh Coriander

Informal supper
Preparation time 15 minutes
Serves 4

675 g (1½ lb) (1 small head) cauliflower

2 tablespoons extra virgin olive oil

4 garlic cloves, thinly sliced

1 teaspoon ground coriander

1 teaspoon salt

½ teaspoon freshly ground five-pepper mixture or black pepper

2 teaspoons finely grated lemon zest

150 ml (5 fl oz) Chicken Stock (see page 134) or vegetable stock, or water

3 tablespoons finely chopped fresh coriander (cilantro)

Curry-flavoured Oil (see page 136), to serve (optional)

Cauliflower, that satisfying vegetable, is not only easy to prepare but is adaptable to almost any type of seasoning. Here, I simply stir-fry it with olive oil and finish it with a shower of fresh coriander.

1 Cut the cauliflower into small florets about 4 cm (1½ inches) wide.

2 Heat a wok or large frying pan over a high heat and add the olive oil. When it is hot and smoking, add the garlic and stir-fry for about 20 seconds to flavour the oil. Quickly add the cauliflower florets and stir-fry them for a few seconds.

3 Add the ground coriander, salt, pepper, lemon zest and stock or water. Reduce the heat and simmer for 10 minutes or until the cauliflower is tender. Stir in the fresh coriander, turn on to a warm serving platter and serve at once, drizzled with curry-flavoured oil, if you wish.

70 Hong Kong-style Broccoli and Baby Corn

East meets West
Preparation time 40 minutes
Serves 4

450 g (1 lb) (2 heads) broccoli

225 g (8 oz) (1 cup) baby corn

4 tablespoons Chinese dried mushrooms

1½ tablespoons groundnut (peanut) oil

1 teaspoon salt

½ teaspoon freshly ground black pepper

1 teaspoon sugar

1 tablespoon Shaoxing rice wine or dry sherry

1 tablespoon light soy sauce

3 tablespoons oyster sauce or dark soy sauce

2 teaspoons sesame oil

Innovation is a virtue in Hong Kong cuisine and chefs there are quick to adopt non-traditional vegetables in their repertoire. In this case, we find broccoli, flown in fresh daily from California, and baby corn, flown in from Thailand. Put them together with traditional Chinese seasonings and flavourings and you have a colourful blend of East and West – so easy to prepare in your wok and serve as a side dish. If you use dark soy sauce instead of oyster sauce, this dish is perfect for vegetarians.

1 Separate the broccoli heads into small florets, then peel and slice the stems. Blanch the broccoli pieces and baby corn in a large pan of boiling salted water for 3 minutes and then immerse them in cold water. Drain thoroughly.

2 Soak the mushrooms in warm water for 20 minutes, then drain them and squeeze out the excess liquid. Remove and discard the stems and finely shred the caps.

3 Heat a wok or large frying pan over a high heat and add the oil. When it is very hot and slightly smoking, add the broccoli, corn and mushrooms and stir-fry for 3 minutes.

4 Add the salt, pepper, sugar, rice wine or dry sherry, light soy sauce and oyster sauce or dark soy sauce and continue to stir-fry at a moderate to high heat for 2 minutes, until the vegetables are thoroughly heated through. Add the sesame oil and stir-fry for 30 seconds, then transfer to a warm platter and serve at once.

71 Ginger–Garlic Carrots

Informal supper
Preparation time 25 minutes
Serves 4

450 g (1 lb) carrots

1 tablespoon groundnut (peanut) oil

3 tablespoons coarsely chopped garlic

1 tablespoon finely chopped fresh root ginger

3–4 tablespoons water

2 tablespoons finely chopped fresh coriander (cilantro)

2 tablespoons finely chopped spring onions (scallions)

salt and ground black pepper

I find carrots that are simply boiled and slathered with butter rather boring, as do most children. No wonder they don't eat their carrots. However, when they are stir-fried in a hot wok, the carrots acquire a smoky flavour that makes them infinitely more appealing. Here is a simple recipe that will have not only children but adults asking for more.

1 Peel the carrots and slice them thinly at a slight diagonal.

2 Heat a wok or large frying pan over a high heat and add the oil. When it is hot, add the garlic and ginger and stir-fry for 20 seconds, until browned. Then quickly add the carrots and stir-fry for 2 minutes longer. Season with salt and pepper.

3 Add the water and stir-fry for 4 minutes or until the carrots are tender and browned. Stir in the coriander and spring onions and serve.

72 Stir-fried Hoisin Turnips

Informal supper
Preparation time 20 minutes
Serves 4

1 tablespoon groundnut (peanut) oil

2 tablespoons thinly sliced garlic

450 g (1 lb) (3 cups) turnips, finely sliced

3 tablespoons hoisin sauce

1 tablespoon dark soy sauce

2 teaspoons sugar

3 tablespoons water

Turnips are a delicious earthy vegetable, often overlooked by home cooks. Here is a quick and simple recipe with the sweet, gentle flavour of hoisin sauce.

1 Heat a wok or large frying pan until it is hot, then add the oil and garlic. Stir-fry for 10 seconds, until the garlic is lightly browned.

2 Add the turnips and stir-fry for 2 minutes, then add the hoisin sauce, soy sauce, sugar and water. Turn the heat to low, cover and cook for 5 minutes or until the turnips are tender. Turn on to a platter and serve at once.

73 Cucumber with Hot Spices

Hot and spicy
Preparation time 40 minutes
Serves 4

675 g (1½ lb) (about 3) small cucumbers

2 teaspoons salt

1 tablespoon groundnut (peanut) oil

1½ tablespoons finely chopped garlic

1½ tablespoons coarsely chopped salted black beans

1 tablespoon finely chopped fresh root ginger

2 tablespoons finely chopped spring onions (scallions)

2 teaspoons chilli bean sauce

1 teaspoon salt

½ teaspoon freshly ground black pepper

2 teaspoons sugar

120 ml (4 fl oz) water

2 teaspoons sesame oil

As a child, I was always surprised to see Americans eating cucumbers raw. We Chinese rarely eat them like this. If they are not pickled, then they must be cooked. We prefer them when they are in season: young, tender and bursting with juice.

This is a simple stir-fried cucumber dish from western China. Once the ingredients are assembled, it is very quick to cook. The chilli and garlic contrast well with the cool, crisp cucumber. If you get into the habit of cooking cucumbers, you will be delighted by their transformation into a true vegetable.

1 Peel the cucumbers, slice them lengthways in half and, using a teaspoon, remove the seeds. Cut the cucumber halves into 2.5 cm (1 inch) cubes. Sprinkle them with the salt and mix well, then place in a colander and leave to drain for 20 minutes. This rids the cucumber of any excess liquid. When the cubes have drained, rinse them in water and blot dry with kitchen paper.

2 Heat a wok or large frying pan until it is very hot and add the groundnut oil. When it is very hot and slightly smoking, add the garlic, black beans, ginger and spring onions and stir-fry for about 30 seconds.

3 Add the cucumbers, chilli bean sauce, salt, pepper and sugar and stir for another 30 seconds, until the cucumber is well coated with the spices and flavourings.

4 Add the water and continue to stir-fry over a high heat for 3–4 minutes, until most of the water has evaporated and the cucumbers are cooked. Mix in the sesame oil and serve at once.

74 Fennel with Garlic

East meets West
Preparation time 10 minutes
Serves 4–6

450 g (1 lb) fennel

1½ tablespoons groundnut (peanut) oil

4 garlic cloves, crushed

1 teaspoon salt

225 g (8 oz) (1 cup) red peppers (bell peppers), deseeded and cut into strips

2 tablespoons water

During my frequent visits to the UK, I like to cook 'Chinese/English' for friends. On such occasions I always prepare vegetables in season. I recently discovered that fennel is delicious stir-fried. I had, of course, long been familiar with its liquorice-flavoured herbal qualities. But even though I knew it as a popular ingredient in the South of France and in Italy, I had never prepared it as a vegetable dish. Serve it with a quick grilled chop and you have a very satisfying meal.

1 Trim the fennel and quarter it, separating the layers

2 Heat a wok or large frying pan and add the oil, garlic and salt. Stir-fry for 10 seconds, then add the fennel, red peppers and water. Continue to stir-fry for 5 minutes or until the vegetables are cooked through, if necessary adding more water to keep them from burning. Serve at once.

75 Stir-fried Chinese Greens

Classic Chinese
Preparation time 10 minutes
Serves 4

1 tablespoon groundnut (peanut) oil

3 garlic cloves, finely sliced

2 teaspoons salt

675 g (1½ lb) (6 cups) Chinese greens, such as Chinese flowering cabbage or *bok choy*

2 tablespoons Chicken Stock (see page 134) or water

Chinese greens are also known by their Cantonese name, *bok choy*. They were a staple food in my childhood, as they were inexpensive, nutritious and readily available. Even today I look forward to this simple stir-fried dish. Sometimes the greens are merely blanched but I think they are delicious stir-fried with oil and garlic or with a little soy sauce and stock. They make a wonderful dish to serve with meat and fish and are excellent as part of a vegetarian meal. You can get Chinese greens at Chinese grocer's shops, but Swiss chard (silverbeet) or mangetout (snowpeas) work equally well.

1 Heat a wok or large frying pan until it is very hot and add the oil. When it is very hot and slightly smoking, add the garlic and salt. Stir-fry for 15 seconds, then add the Chinese greens. Stir-fry for 3–4 minutes, until the greens have wilted a little.

2 Add the chicken stock or water and stir-fry for a few more minutes, until the greens are tender but still slightly crisp.

76 Broad Beans with Red Curry

Easy entertaining
Preparation time 25 minutes
Serves 2–4

900 g (2 lb) (4 cups) fresh broad (lima) beans, unshelled or 350 g (12 oz) (1½ cups) frozen broad (lima) beans

1 tablespoon groundnut (peanut) oil

3 tablespoons finely sliced garlic

3 tablespoons finely sliced shallots

2 small, fresh red Thai chilli peppers, deseeded and sliced

2 teaspoons sugar

2 teaspoons Thai red curry paste

1 tablespoon fish sauce (*nam pla*) or light soy sauce

2 tablespoons water

freshly ground black pepper

Buttery, succulent broad beans are a favourite throughout Asia. In Thailand they are stir-fried with red curry paste, which gives them a rich and refreshing dimension without masking their distinctive qualities. This dish, called *thua pak-a-phad prig daeng*, makes an impressive and delicious side dish or first course (appetizer). Broad beans are, of course, best eaten as fresh as can be, but frozen beans are a very acceptable substitute.

1 If you are using fresh broad beans, shell them and then blanch in a large pan of boiling salted water for 2 minutes. Drain thoroughly, refresh in cold water and drain again. When cool, slip off the skins. If you are using frozen beans, simply thaw them.

2 Heat a wok or large frying pan over a high heat and add the oil. When it is very hot and slightly smoking, add the garlic, shallots, chilli peppers and some black pepper and stir-fry for 1 minute.

3 Add the broad beans, sugar, red curry paste, fish sauce and water and continue to stir-fry over a high heat for 2 minutes. Serve at once.

77 Bright Pepper and Green Bean Stir-fry

Light and fresh
Preparation time 10 minutes
Serves 4–6

225 g (8 oz) (2 large) red peppers (bell peppers)

1½ tablespoons groundnut (peanut) oil

2 tablespoons coarsely chopped garlic

1½ teaspoons salt

225 g (8 oz) (1 cup) French (green) beans, trimmed

1 teaspoon sugar

2 tablespoons water

Red peppers and green beans, nicely seasoned, combine to form a colourful and nutritious salad that is appropriate for any meal. This dish is also good served at room temperature.

1 Deseed the peppers and cut them into strips.

2 Heat a wok or large frying pan and add the oil. Add the garlic, salt, peppers and French beans and stir-fry for 2 minutes. Then add the sugar and water and cook for another 4 minutes or until the vegetables are tender. Serve at once.

78 Spinach with Garlic

Classic Chinese
Preparation time 10 minutes
Serves 4

675 g (1½ lb) (6 cups) fresh spinach

1 tablespoon groundnut (peanut) oil

1 tablespoon finely chopped garlic

1 teaspoon salt

1 teaspoon sugar

Spinach is often regarded with disdain in the West, probably because it is usually overcooked. This is a delicious, time-honoured, southern Chinese recipe. The spinach is quickly stir-fried and then seasoned. It is very simple to prepare.

1 Wash the spinach thoroughly and remove all the stalks, leaving just the leaves. Set aside.

2 Heat a wok or large frying pan until it is very hot and then add the oil. When it is very hot and slightly smoking, add the garlic and salt and stir-fry for 10 seconds. Then add the spinach and stir-fry for about 2 minutes to coat the leaves thoroughly with the oil, garlic and salt.

3 When the spinach has wilted to about a third of its original volume, add the sugar and stir-fry for another 4 minutes. Transfer to a plate and pour off any excess liquid. Serve hot or cold.

79 Stir-fried Singapore Water Spinach

Informal supper
Preparation time 20 minutes
Serves 2–4

675 g (1½ lb) (6 cups) water spinach or regular spinach

2 tablespoons groundnut (peanut) oil

2 teaspoons shrimp paste

50 g (2 oz) (¼ cup) shallots, finely sliced

5 garlic cloves, finely sliced

2 fresh red chilli peppers, deseeded and chopped

1 teaspoon sugar

salt and freshly ground black pepper

My good friend Jenny Lo, who is Malaysian–Chinese, introduced me to this delicious, earthy dish. I have since eaten it numerous times in Singapore. Water spinach is a leafy vegetable that is prolific throughout south-east Asia. It is similar to ordinary spinach, which can easily be substituted. However, the appeal of water spinach is the crunchy, hollow stalk, that is just as tasty as the leaves. You can find water spinach in Chinese supermarkets and groceries.

1 If you are using water spinach, wash it thoroughly and trim any tough ends off the stalks. If you are using ordinary spinach, wash it thoroughly and remove and discard the stalks.

2 Heat a wok or large frying pan over a high heat and add the oil. When it is very hot and slightly smoking, add the shrimp paste and crush it in the hot oil. Add the shallots and garlic and stir-fry for 2–3 minutes, until they are lightly browned.

3 Add the chilli peppers, sugar and spinach. Stir-fry for about 2 minutes to coat the spinach thoroughly with the aromatic mixture.

4 After the spinach has wilted to about a third of its original volume, stir-fry for another 4 minutes. Season with salt and pepper, then transfer the spinach to a plate and pour off any excess liquid. Serve immediately.

80 Spicy Stir-fried Mushrooms

| Hot and spicy |
| Preparation time 20 minutes |
| Serves 4 |

1 tablespoon groundnut
(peanut) oil

2 teaspoons finely chopped
garlic

2 teaspoons finely chopped
fresh root ginger

1 tablespoon finely chopped
spring onions (scallions)

450 g (1 lb) (4 cups) small
button mushrooms, trimmed

2 teaspoons chilli bean sauce

1 tablespoon Shaoxing rice
wine or dry sherry

2 teaspoons dark soy sauce

1 teaspoon salt

1/2 teaspoon freshly ground
black pepper

1 tablespoon Chicken Stock
(see page 134) or water

2 teaspoons sugar

2 teaspoons sesame oil

Although button mushrooms are common in Europe and America, they were virtually unknown in China until quite recently. They are now increasingly popular there. Their mild, subtle flavour makes them perfect for stir-frying with Chinese spices. This dish reheats well. It goes perfectly with grilled (broiled) meat.

1 Heat a wok or large frying pan until it is very hot and add the groundnut oil. When it is very hot and slightly smoking, add the garlic, ginger and spring onions and stir-fry for about 20 seconds. Add the mushrooms and stir-fry them for about 30 seconds.

2 Quickly add all the rest of the ingredients except for the sesame oil. Stir-fry for about 5 minutes or until the mushrooms are cooked through and have absorbed all the spices and seasonings.

3 Just before serving, add the sesame oil and give the mixture a couple of quick stirs. Turn it on to a warm serving dish and serve at once, as the mushrooms are particularly delicious when hot.

81 Cloud Ears Stir-fried with Mangetout

Easy entertaining
Preparation time 40 minutes
Serves 4

15 g (½ oz) (1 tablespoon) Chinese dried cloud ears

1 tablespoon groundnut (peanut) oil

2 garlic cloves, crushed

100 g (4 oz) (½ cup) celery, sliced on the diagonal

225 g (8 oz) (1 cup) mangetout (snowpeas), trimmed

100 g (4 oz) (½ cup) water chestnuts (peeled if fresh, rinsed if canned), sliced

FOR THE SAUCE:

1 tablespoon oyster sauce

1 teaspoon light soy sauce

2 teaspoons dark soy sauce

1 teaspoon sugar

2 teaspoons Shaoxing rice wine or dry sherry

2 teaspoons sesame oil

150 ml (5 fl oz) Chicken Stock (see page 134) or vegetable stock

2 teaspoons cornflour (cornstarch), blended with 2 teaspoons water

This is a colourful and wholesome vegetable dish that is easily assembled for a family dinner. It is a classic combination of the tastes and textures so typical of Chinese cookery. The cloud ears have little flavour of their own but, like mushrooms in general, they readily absorb other flavours and retain their chewy texture. And, like truffles in French cuisine, cloud ears enhance an entire recipe, bringing out the best in the other ingredients.

1 Soak the cloud ears in warm water for 20 minutes, until soft, then drain and set aside.

2 Heat a wok or large frying pan over a medium heat and add the oil. When hot, add the garlic and stir-fry for 30 seconds. Then add the cloud ears and celery and stir-fry for 2 minutes. Stir in the mangetout and the water chestnuts if using fresh ones, and stir-fry for another minute.

3 Add all the sauce ingredients except the blended cornflour. Bring the sauce to the boil and then stir in the cornflour mixture. If you are using canned water chestnuts, add them at this stage and warm through. Turn the mixture on to a serving platter and serve at once.

82 Stir-fried Mushrooms Provençal

East meets West
Preparation time 15 minutes
Serves 2–4

2 tablespoons extra virgin olive oil

2 tablespoons coarsely chopped garlic

450 g (1 lb) (4 cups) button mushrooms, sliced

4 tablespoons finely chopped fresh flat-leaf parsley

2 tablespoons finely chopped fresh chives

2 tablespoons finely chopped spring onions (scallions)

salt and freshly ground black pepper

This simple stir-fried recipe was inspired by Bruna Taurines. She is a fabulous cook, originally from Italy, but who has lived most of her life in Provence. It was there, in Martigues, that I discovered the extraordinary combination of parsley and garlic. I have, of course, added my own personal touches but I owe my inspiration in this recipe to her cooking.

1 Place a wok or large frying pan over a high heat until it is moderately hot. Add the olive oil, then immediately add the garlic and stir-fry for 15 seconds.

2 Add the mushrooms and some salt and pepper and stir-fry for 5–7 minutes or until the mushroom liquid has been reabsorbed by the mushrooms.

3 Add the chopped parsley, chives and spring onions and cook for 2 minutes. Give the mushrooms a few stirs, turn on to a warm platter and serve at once.

83 Stir-fried Five-Spice Vegetables

Informal supper
Preparation time 25 minutes
Serves 4–6

100 g (4 oz) carrots

100 g (4 oz) canned bamboo shoots

100 g (4 oz) courgettes (zucchini)

100 g (4 oz) celery heart

100 g (4 oz) (about 1) red or green pepper (bell pepper)

1½ tablespoons groundnut (peanut) oil

1 tablespoon coarsely chopped garlic

3 tablespoons finely chopped shallots

3 tablespoons finely chopped spring onions (scallions)

2 teaspoons light soy sauce

2 teaspoons Shaoxing rice wine or dry sherry

2 teaspoons five-spice powder

salt and freshly ground black pepper

It is amazing how easily simple vegetables can be elevated to a tasty treat with a dash of five-spice powder. Here, a colourful mixture of vegetables is stir-fried in the wok for a crunchy and delicious vegetarian dish that will also satisfy non-vegetarians.

1 Peel the carrots and cut them into fine shreds 5 cm (2 inches) long. Cut the bamboo shoots, courgettes, celery heart and pepper into shreds of the same size.

2 Heat a wok or large frying pan over a high heat and add the oil. When it is very hot and slightly smoking, add the garlic, shallots and spring onions and stir-fry for 20 seconds. Then add the carrots and stir-fry for another minute.

3 Add the remaining vegetables, plus the soy sauce, rice wine or dry sherry, five-spice powder and some salt and pepper. Stir-fry the mixture for 3 minutes, then turn on to a platter and serve at once.

84 Rainbow Vegetables

<table>
<tr><td>Easy entertaining</td></tr>
<tr><td>Preparation time 60 minutes</td></tr>
<tr><td>Serves 4–6</td></tr>
</table>

15 g (½ oz) (1 tablespoon) Chinese dried mushrooms

100 g (4 oz) each of:
carrots
canned bamboo shoots
courgettes (zucchini)
celery heart
pressed, seasoned beancurd (tofu)

1 red or green pepper (bell pepper)

½ head iceberg lettuce

1½ tablespoons groundnut (peanut) oil

1 tablespoon chopped garlic

3 tablespoons finely chopped shallots

3 tablespoons finely chopped spring onions (scallions)

2 teaspoons light soy sauce

2 teaspoons Shaoxing rice wine or dry sherry

3 tablespoons vegetarian oyster-flavoured sauce or dark soy sauce

salt and freshly ground five-pepper mixture

TO SERVE:

4 tablespoons hoisin sauce

25 g (1 oz) bean thread (transparent) noodles, deep-fried (optional)

Whoever said vegetarian food has to be dreary and boring was manifesting a lack of imagination and a deficiency in the art of cookery. For example, here is a delicious vegetarian treat, appealing to the eye as well as the palate. The colourful vegetables constitute the 'rainbow', and they are stir-fried and served with crisp lettuce and hoisin sauce to create an unusual combination of tastes and textures. I use bought pressed, seasoned beancurd as a meat substitute.

This dish also makes a good finger-food appetizer for a dinner party. The rainbow vegetable mixture and lettuce leaves are served on individual platters, and the hoisin sauce in a small bowl. Each guest puts a helping of each ingredient into a hollow lettuce leaf, rather like stuffing a pancake or a taco, and eats the filled leaf with his or her fingers. As an extra, you can also deep-fry bean thread noodles and serve them on top of the rainbow vegetables.

1 Soak the dried mushrooms in warm water for 20 minutes, then drain them and squeeze out any excess liquid. Trim off the stems and shred the caps into strips 5 cm (2 inches) long.

2 Peel the carrots. Cut the carrots, bamboo shoots, courgettes and pepper into fine shreds 5 cm (2 inches) long. Finely shred the celery heart and pressed beancurd. Separate and wash the lettuce leaves, spin them in a salad spinner and refrigerate until needed.

3 Heat a wok or large frying pan over a high heat and add the oil. When it is very hot and slightly smoking, add the finely chopped garlic, shallots and spring onions and stir-fry for 20 seconds. Then add the carrots and stir-fry for another minute.

4 Add all the remaining vegetables (except the lettuce), plus the soy sauce, rice wine or sherry, oyster sauce, salt and pepper. Stir-fry the mixture for 3 minutes, then turn on to a platter.

5 Arrange the lettuce leaves on a separate platter. Put the hoisin sauce into a small bowl, the bean thread noodles, if using, in another bowl, and serve at once.

85 Mock Vegetable Pasta

Light and fresh
Preparation time 45 minutes
Serves 4

900 g (2 lb) courgettes (zucchini)

1 tablespoon salt

1 tablespoon groundnut (peanut) oil

1 tablespoon finely chopped garlic

2 teaspoons finely chopped fresh root ginger

2 tablespoons finely chopped fresh coriander (cilantro)

2 tablespoons finely chopped spring onions (scallions), green part only

In Chinese vegetarian cookery, a dish is not always what it appears to be. For example, 'mock duck' is taro root stuffed with finely chopped vegetables and fried to a golden brown to look like duck. I enjoy the fun and imagination in such creativity. Here I take courgettes and cut them into long, thin strips to look like pasta, then I salt them to remove excess moisture and, in the process, firm their texture. Quickly stir-fried with traditional Chinese seasonings, the resulting dish looks and tastes like pasta. My guests are always surprised by its lightness, flavour and texture.

Do not overcook the courgettes – you want *al dente* firmness. This mock pasta is delicious cold, and it can also function as a vegetable or salad serving. It is perfect for picnics, too.

1 Cut the courgettes into long, thin strips resembling pasta. Put the strips into a colander and sprinkle with the salt. Leave to stand for 20 minutes, then wrap the courgettes in a kitchen towel and squeeze out the excess liquid.

2 Heat a wok or large frying pan over a moderate heat and add the oil. Put in the garlic and ginger and stir-fry for 30 seconds.

3 Add the courgettes, coriander and spring onions and continue to stir-fry for 4 minutes or until the courgettes are heated through. Turn the mixture on to a platter and serve warm or at room temperature.

86 Spicy Orange-flavoured Beancurd

East meets West
Preparation time 40 minutes
Serves 4

900 g (2 lb) (4 cups) firm, fresh beancurd (tofu)

3 tablespoons groundnut (peanut) oil

10 dried red chilli peppers, halved

450 g (1 lb) (2½ cups) onions, coarsely sliced

4 tablespoons shredded orange zest

2 tablespoons coarsely chopped garlic

4 tablespoons Shaoxing rice wine or dry sherry

4 tablespoons dark soy sauce

½ teaspoon freshly ground five-pepper mixture or black pepper

2 teaspoons sugar

4 teaspoons sesame oil

Le Cheval is a deservedly popular Vietnamese restaurant in Oakland, California, but, as its name suggests, it also reflects a French *esprit de finesse* along with its native culinary inventiveness. It offers a variety of beancurd dishes, which are luscious and satisfying. This spicy, orange-flavoured beancurd is among the most delectable on the menu, with an East–West Fusion touch. The beancurd is lightly fried in oil and then finished off with aromatic fresh orange zest, onions and rice wine, with dried chilli peppers adding their pleasant bite. This recipe will serve 4 as a main course (entrée).

1 Cut the beancurd into 2.5 cm (1 inch) cubes and leave to drain on kitchen paper for 20 minutes.

2 Heat a wok or large frying pan over a high heat and add the groundnut oil. When it is very hot and slightly smoking, add the dried chilli peppers and stir-fry for 20 seconds.

3 Push the chilli peppers to the side of the wok or pan, turn the temperature down, add the beancurd cubes and brown slowly on all sides. When the cubes are golden brown all over, remove the beancurd and chilli peppers and drain on kitchen paper.

4 Add the onions, orange zest and garlic to the wok or pan and stir-fry for 3 minutes, until the onions have wilted. Now add the rice wine or sherry, soy sauce, pepper and sugar. Return the browned beancurd cubes to the wok or pan and stir-fry for 3 minutes.

5 Add the sesame oil and turn the mixture gently several times to mix well. Serve at once, or allow to cool, then reheat when ready to serve.

87 Stir-fried Mixed Vegetables

Informal supper
Preparation time 15 minutes
Serves 4

225 g (8 oz) (1 head) broccoli

225 g (8 oz) asparagus

225 g (8 oz) (1 cup) Chinese leaves (Chinese cabbage)

225 g (8 oz) (1 cup) fresh or canned baby sweetcorn

2 tablespoons groundnut (peanut) oil

3 tablespoons finely sliced garlic

3 tablespoons finely sliced shallots

2 small, fresh red Thai chilli peppers, deseeded and sliced

1½ tablespoons fish sauce (*nam pla*)

2 tablespoons oyster sauce

2 teaspoons sugar

1 teaspoon salt

This is a colourful and delicious offering. An assortment of vegetables is suggested below but you may choose your own favourites. When stir-frying, remember to begin with the firmer vegetables, which will need more cooking.

This dish is known as *phad phag ruam mit* in Thailand. To make a vegetarian version, simply use vegetarian oyster sauce (which is made with mushrooms) and substitute light soy sauce for the fish sauce.

1 Divide the broccoli into florets. Peel the stalks and slice them thinly on the diagonal. Trim the woody ends of the asparagus and then cut into 4 cm (1½ inch) lengths. Cut the Chinese leaves into 4 cm (1½ inch) strips.

2 Blanch the sweetcorn and broccoli in a large pan of boiling salted water for 3 minutes. Drain well and then plunge them into cold water to stop them cooking further.

3 Heat a wok or large frying pan over a high heat until it is medium hot. Add the oil and garlic and stir-fry for 1–1½ minutes, until the garlic is golden brown. Remove with a slotted spoon and place on kitchen paper to drain. Now add the shallots and chilli peppers to the wok and stir-fry for 1 minute.

4 Add the corn and asparagus and stir-fry for 30 seconds. Add the fish sauce and bring the mixture to the boil, then cover and cook over a high heat for 2 minutes.

5 Add the broccoli and Chinese leaves, together with the oyster sauce, sugar and salt. Continue cooking over a high heat for 3 minutes or until the vegetables are tender. Turn on to a platter, garnish with the fried garlic and serve at once.

88 Chow Mein

Classic Chinese
Preparation time 20 minutes
Serves 4

225 g (8 oz) egg noodles

4 teaspoons sesame oil

100 g (4 oz) boneless, skinless chicken breasts, cut into fine shreds 5 cm (2 inches) long

2¹⁄₂ tablespoons groundnut (peanut) oil

1 tablespoon finely chopped garlic

50 g (2 oz) (¹⁄₄ cup) mangetout (snowpeas), finely shredded

4 slices Parma ham or 2 slices cooked ham, finely shredded

2 teaspoons light soy sauce

2 teaspoons dark soy sauce

1 tablespoon Shaoxing rice wine or dry sherry

1 teaspoon salt

¹⁄₂ teaspoon freshly ground white pepper

¹⁄₂ teaspoon sugar

3 tablespoons finely chopped spring onions (scallions)

FOR THE MARINADE:

2 teaspoons light soy sauce

2 teaspoons Shaoxing rice wine or dry sherry

1 teaspoon sesame oil

¹⁄₂ teaspoon salt

¹⁄₂ teaspoon freshly ground white pepper

Chow mein literally means 'stir-fried noodles' and this dish is as popular in the West as it is in southern China. It is a quick and delicious way to prepare egg noodles. Almost any ingredient you like, such as fish, meat, poultry or vegetables, can be added. It makes a popular lunch dish, either served at the end of the meal or eaten by itself. You can use the same quantity of dried or fresh egg noodles.

1 Cook the noodles in a large pan of boiling water for 3–5 minutes, then drain and plunge them into cold water. Drain thoroughly, toss them with 3 teaspoons of the sesame oil and set aside.

2 Combine the chicken shreds with all the marinade ingredients, mix well and then leave to marinate for about 10 minutes.

3 Heat a wok over a high heat. Add 1 tablespoon of the groundnut oil and, when it is very hot and slightly smoking, add the chicken shreds. Stir-fry for about 2 minutes and then transfer to a plate. Wipe the wok clean.

4 Reheat the wok until it is very hot, then add the remaining groundnut oil. When the oil is slightly smoking, add the garlic and stir-fry for 10 seconds. Then add the mangetout and ham and stir-fry for about 1 minute.

5 Add the noodles, soy sauces, rice wine or sherry, salt, pepper, sugar and spring onions. Stir-fry for 2 minutes.

6 Return the chicken and any juices to the noodle mixture. Stir-fry for 3–4 minutes or until the chicken is cooked. Add the remaining sesame oil and give the mixture a few final stirs. Turn it on to a warm platter and serve at once.

89 Stir-fried Vegetables over a Rice Noodle Cloud

Easy entertaining
Preparation time 45 minutes
Serves 4–6

350 g (12 oz) aubergines (eggplant)

225 g (8 oz) courgettes (zucchini)

300 ml (10 fl oz) groundnut (peanut) oil

175 g (6 oz) rice noodles, rice vermicelli or rice sticks

3 garlic cloves, crushed

4 spring onions (scallions), chopped

2 tablespoons Shaoxing rice wine or dry sherry

2 tablespoons yellow bean sauce

2 teaspoons chilli bean sauce

150 ml (5 fl oz) Chicken Stock (see page 134) or vegetable stock

1 teaspoon sugar

2 tablespoons dark soy sauce

1 teaspoon salt

1 teaspoon cornflour (cornstarch), blended with 1 teaspoon water

At Chinese banquets when I was a child, the food we children enjoyed most were the dishes that featured fried rice noodles. I believe this is still true today for Western children whose parents take them to Chinese restaurants. Practically any stir-fried dish with a little sauce makes a wonderful topping for these crisp, crackling, crunchy noodles. In this recipe, I combine them with slightly spiced vegetables, enhanced with aromatic seasonings.

1 Cut the aubergines and courgettes into 7.5 cm (3 inch) batons. Sprinkle them with salt and leave in a sieve to drain for 20 minutes. Rinse under cold running water and pat dry with kitchen paper.

2 Heat the oil in a deep-fat fryer or large wok. Add the noodles and deep-fry until they are crisp and puffed up. Remove with a slotted spoon and drain on kitchen paper. You may have to do this in several batches.

3 Heat a wok or large frying pan and add 1½ tablespoons of the oil in which you fried the noodles. When moderately hot, add the garlic and spring onions and stir-fry for 30 seconds. Add the aubergines and courgettes and continue to stir-fry for 1 minute.

4 Stir in all the rest of the ingredients except the cornflour mixture and cook for 3 minutes. Finally, add the blended cornflour and cook for a minute longer.

5 Place the deep-fried noodles on a platter and spoon the vegetables over the top. Serve immediately.

90 Spicy Sichuan Noodles

Hot and spicy
Preparation time 50 minutes
Serves 4

225 g (8 oz) minced (ground) fatty pork

450 g (1 lb) dried or fresh Chinese egg noodles

1 tablespoon sesame oil

2 tablespoons groundnut (peanut) oil

2 tablespoons finely chopped garlic

2 tablespoons finely chopped fresh root ginger

5 tablespoons finely chopped spring onions (scallions)

2 tablespoons sesame paste or smooth peanut butter

2 tablespoons dark soy sauce

2 teaspoons light soy sauce

2 teaspoons chilli bean sauce

2 tablespoons Chilli Oil (see page 137)

Salt and ground black pepper

250 ml (8 fl oz) Chicken Stock (see page 134)

2 teaspoons Sichuan pepper-corns, roasted and freshly ground (see page 140)

FOR THE MARINADE:

1 tablespoon dark soy sauce

2 teaspoons Shaoxing rice wine or dry sherry

Salt and ground black pepper

This is a typical Sichuan dish. Although it is spicy and pungent, it is nevertheless popular throughout China, especially in the north. Such noodle dishes – *xiao chi*, or 'small eats' – are found in hole-in-the-wall restaurants, food stalls and other commercial spots offering snacks. There are many versions of the dish and they are all easy to make, tasty and quite filling. This is my version of this delightful noodle dish.

1 Combine the pork with all the marinade ingredients in a bowl and mix well. Leave to marinate for 20 minutes.

2 Cook the noodles in a large pan of boiling water for 3–5 minutes, then drain and plunge them into cold water. Drain thoroughly and toss them in the sesame oil. (They can be kept in this state, tightly covered with cling film (plastic wrap), for up to 2 hours in the refrigerator.)

3 Heat a wok or large frying pan until it is very hot and add the groundnut oil. When it is very hot and slightly smoking, add the garlic, ginger and spring onions and stir-fry for 30 seconds. Then add the pork mixture and continue to stir-fry until the pork loses its pink colour.

4 Add all the remaining ingredients except the Sichuan peppercorns and cook for 2 minutes. Now add the noodles, mixing well. Turn the mixture on to a warm serving platter, sprinkle with the ground peppercorns and serve at once.

91 Singapore Noodles

Easy entertaining
Preparation time 45 minutes
Serves 4–6

225 g (8 oz) thin rice noodles

50 g (2 oz) (4 tablespoons) Chinese dried mushrooms

175 g (6 oz) (1 cup) frozen small garden peas or petits pois

4 eggs, beaten

1 tablespoon sesame oil

1 teaspoon salt

1/2 teaspoon freshly ground white pepper

3 tablespoons groundnut (peanut) oil

1 1/2 tablespoons finely chopped garlic

1 tablespoon finely chopped fresh root ginger

6 fresh red or green chilli peppers, deseeded and finely shredded

6 water chestnuts, peeled if fresh, rinsed if canned

100 g (4 oz) (3/4 cup) Chinese barbecue pork or cooked ham, finely shredded

3 spring onions (scallions), finely shredded

100 g (4 oz) small cooked prawns (shrimp), peeled

fresh coriander leaves (cilantro), to garnish

Curry is not original to Chinese cuisine. It was introduced to China centuries ago by immigrants returning home from sojourns in Southeast Asia, especially from the East Coast of India. This is why, even today, curry continues to be popular in south and eastern China, the regions that had the most returning immigrants from faraway Singapore. Chinese cuisine readily adopts new foods and ingredients when their virtues are recognised, as in the case of curry.

These light and subtle rice noodles are an ideal foil for the spicy sauce. A bonus is that they are easy to prepare. Serve with a fish or meat dish, or just by themselves. If rice noodles are unavailable, substitute Chinese egg noodles. This dish is also wonderful cold and would make a lovely and unusual picnic offering. For a vegetarian version, just omit the meat and prawns and use more coconut milk – another adopted food – in place of chicken stock.

1 Soak the rice noodles in a bowl of warm water for 25 minutes, then drain them in a colander or sieve. (If you are using dried egg noodles, cook them in a pan of boiling water for 3–5 minutes, then drain and plunge into cold water. Drain thoroughly and toss them in a tablespoon of groundnut oil.) Set the noodles aside until you are ready to use them.

2 Soak the mushrooms in warm water for 20 minutes, then drain and squeeze out the excess liquid. Remove and discard the stems and shred the caps into thin strips.

3 Put the peas in a small bowl and let them thaw. Combine the eggs with the sesame oil, salt and pepper and set aside.

4 Heat a wok or large frying pan until it is very hot and add the groundnut oil. When it is very hot and slightly smoking, add the garlic, ginger and chilli peppers and stir-fry for 30 seconds. Add the water chestnuts, mushrooms, pork or ham and spring onions, then stir-fry for 1 minute.

5 Add the rice noodles, prawns and peas and stir-fry for 2 minutes. Now add all the sauce ingredients and continue to cook over a high heat for another 5 minutes or until most of the liquid has evaporated.

(continued opposite)

FOR THE CURRY SAUCE:

2 tablespoons light soy sauce

3 tablespoons Indian Madras curry paste or 2 tablespoons curry powder

2 tablespoons Shaoxing rice wine

1 tablespoon sugar

1 teaspoon salt

1 teaspoon black pepper

250 ml (8 fl oz) canned coconut milk

175 ml (6 fl oz) Chicken Stock (see page 134)

6 Add the egg mixture, stir-frying constantly until the egg has set. Turn the mixture on to a large, warm serving platter, garnish with coriander leaves and serve at once.

92 Quick Curry Noodles

East meets West
Preparation time 10 minutes
Serves 4

350 g (12 oz) dried or fresh Chinese noodles

2 teaspoons sesame oil

3 tablespoons finely chopped fresh chives

FOR THE SAUCE:

3 tablespoons extra virgin olive oil

2 teaspoons sesame oil

3 tablespoons finely chopped shallots

2 tablespoons Dijon mustard

1 tablespoon Madras curry powder

2 tablespoons light soy sauce

1 tablespoon dark soy sauce

salt and ground black pepper

Chinese noodles are perfect for a quick, tasty meal. In this recipe, the noodles are tossed in an unusual East–West sauce of mustard, curry and soy. The bold flavours marry well with the bland noodles.

1 Cook the noodles in a large pan of boiling water for 3–5 minutes, then drain and plunge into cold water. Drain thoroughly and toss them in the sesame oil. (They can be kept in this state, tightly covered with cling film (plastic wrap), for up to 2 hours in the refrigerator.)

2 Heat a wok or large frying pan and add the olive and sesame oil. Immediately add the shallots and stir-fry for 2 minutes, until lightly browned. Then add the mustard, curry powder, soy sauces and some salt and pepper.

3 Toss in the cooked noodles and stir-fry for about 3 minutes, until heated through, mixing well all the while. Add the chives, mix well and serve at once.

93 Korean Bean Thread Sesame Noodles and Vegetables

Informal supper
Preparation time 35 minutes
Serves 4

25 g (1 oz) (2 tablespoons) **Chinese dried mushrooms**

15 g (½ oz) (1 tablespoon) **Chinese dried cloud ears**

100 g (4 oz) (½ cup) **bean thread (transparent) noodles**

2 tablespoons **groundnut (peanut) oil**

50 g (2 oz) (⅜ cup) **carrot, finely shredded**

1 small **onion, finely shredded**

1 **green pepper (bell pepper), finely shredded**

120 ml (4 fl oz) **water**

FOR THE SAUCE:

2 tablespoons **light soy sauce**

2 tablespoons **dark soy sauce**

3 tablespoons **sesame oil**

1½ tablespoons **sesame seeds**

1 tablespoon finely chopped **garlic**

1 tablespoon **sugar**

1 teaspoon **black pepper**

This simple-to-prepare recipe is my own version of a popular Korean dish. What makes it memorable is the combination of lace-like noodles and exotic mushrooms, an unusual mixture of tastes and textures.

1 Soak the dried mushrooms in warm water for 20 minutes, until soft. Squeeze out any excess liquid, then remove and discard the stalks. Cut the caps into shreds.

2 Soak the cloud ears in warm water for 20 minutes or until soft. Rinse well in cold water and drain thoroughly in a colander. Leave whole.

3 Soak the noodles in a large bowl of very hot water for 15 minutes. When soft, drain well. Using scissors or a knife, cut the noodles into 7.5 cm (3 inch) lengths.

4 Heat a wok or large frying pan and add the oil. When it is moderately hot, add the mushrooms, cloud ears, carrot, onion, green pepper and water and stir-fry for 5 minutes or until the carrot is cooked.

5 Combine all the sauce ingredients and add to the vegetables. Give the mixture a good stir, then add the noodles and stir-fry for 2 minutes, until heated through. Serve at once or at room temperature.

94 Stir-fried Rice Noodles

Easy entertaining
Preparation time 50 minutes
Serves 4

225 g (8 oz) wide dried rice noodles

450 g (1 lb) raw prawns (green shrimp)

2 tablespoons salt

3 tablespoons groundnut (peanut) oil

3 tablespoons coarsely chopped garlic

3 tablespoons finely sliced shallots

2 large, fresh red or green chilli peppers, deseeded and chopped

2 eggs, beaten

2 tablespoons lime juice

3 tablespoons fish sauce (*nam pla*)

1 tablespoon Sweet Chilli Sauce (see page 137)

1 teaspoon sugar

¹⁄₂ teaspoon ground black pepper

175 g (6 oz) (1¹⁄₂ cups) bean sprouts

TO GARNISH:

1 lime, cut into wedges

3 tablespoons coarsely chopped fresh coriander (cilantro)

3 spring onions (scallions), sliced

3 tablespoons coarsely chopped roasted peanuts

1 teaspoon dried chilli flakes

Phad thai is probably one of the most popular dishes in Thailand, prepared in homes throughout the country as well as at countless street stalls. It combines the essential Thai flavours of sweet, sour, hot and spicy.

1 Soak the rice noodles in a bowl of warm water for 25 minutes, then drain them in a colander or sieve.

2 Peel the prawns, make a slit down the back of each one and pull out the fine digestive cord with the tip of the knife. Wash the prawns in cold water with a tablespoon of salt, then drain and repeat. Rinse well and pat dry with kitchen paper.

3 Heat a wok or large frying pan over a high heat until it is very hot, then add 1 tablespoon of the oil. When it is very hot and slightly smoking, add the prawns and stir-fry for about 2 minutes. Remove from the pan and set aside.

4 Re-heat the wok, add the remaining oil, then add the garlic, shallots and chilli peppers and stir-fry for 1 minute. Now add the drained noodles and stir-fry for another minute.

5 Add the beaten eggs, lime juice, fish sauce, chilli sauce, sugar and black pepper and stir-fry for 3 minutes. Return the prawns to the wok, toss in the bean sprouts and stir-fry for 2 minutes.

6 Turn the mixture on to a platter, garnish with the lime wedges, coriander, spring onions, peanuts and chilli flakes and serve at once.

95 Angel Hair Pasta with Spicy Tomato Sauce

East meets West
Preparation time 20 minutes
Serves 4–6

900 g (2 lb) (4 cups) fresh or canned tomatoes

150 ml (5 fl oz) extra virgin olive oil

100 g (4 oz) (½ cup) onions, finely chopped

2 tablespoons finely chopped fresh root ginger

3 tablespoons coarsely chopped garlic

3 tablespoons finely chopped spring onions (scallions)

2 tablespoons deseeded and finely chopped red chilli peppers

1 tablespoon chilli bean sauce

1 tablespoon Shaoxing rice wine or dry sherry

2 teaspoons sugar

2 teaspoons salt

1 teaspoon freshly ground black pepper

450 g (1 lb) dried angel hair pasta

TO SERVE:

a small handful of fresh basil leaves

freshly grated Parmesan cheese

Chinese noodles are made from a softer wheat than Italian pasta. However, I have grown to love the *al dente* texture of pasta. Here I have added a spicy twist to this classic Italian dish with a few Asian flavours, which make it even more satisfying to my taste.

This quick and easy recipe is perfect for vegetarians, and may serve as a light lunch or as the centrepiece for a large, informal dinner party.

1 If you are using fresh tomatoes, skin and deseed them, then cut them into 2.5 cm (1 inch) cubes. If you are using canned tomatoes, cut them into small chunks.

2 Heat a wok or large frying pan and add the olive oil. Add the onions, ginger, garlic, spring onions and chilli peppers and stir-fry for 2 minutes. Then add the chilli bean sauce, rice wine or sherry, sugar, salt and pepper and continue to cook for 1 minute.

3 Add the tomatoes, turn the heat to low and simmer gently for 30 minutes. The sauce can be made a day ahead to this point.

4 Cook the pasta in a large pan of boiling salted water until *al dente*. Drain well and add to the sauce in the wok. Mix thoroughly, stir in the basil leaves and serve on a large platter, with freshly grated Parmesan cheese.

96 Stir-fried Fusilli *alla Carbonara*

East meets West
Preparation time 10 minutes
Serves 4

350 g (12 oz) dried fusilli

3 tablespoons olive oil

3 tablespoons coarsely chopped garlic

1 small onion, chopped

2 tablespoons finely grated orange zest

12 thin slices of pancetta (or 12 slices bacon), chopped

2 large eggs, beaten

a handful of fresh chives, chopped

salt and freshly ground black pepper

Stir-frying is a quick and easy way to turn leftovers in your fridge into a delicious and tasty treat. Simply add cooked Italian pasta to the mix and you have a satisfying meal. In this recipe I have added bacon as well as eggs to make my version of pasta *alla carbonara*, without the cream. This recipe makes a fine starter for a multi-course meal or can easily be a main course (entrée) with salad.

1 Cook the pasta in a large pan of boiling salted water until *al dente*, then drain well and set aside.

2 Heat a wok or large frying pan over a high heat and add the olive oil. When it is very hot and slightly smoking, add the garlic, onion and orange zest and stir-fry for 2 minutes. Then add the pancetta or bacon and stir-fry for 3–4 minutes, until browned.

3 Next add the drained pasta and some salt and pepper and stir-fry for 5 minutes over a high heat. Add the beaten eggs and stir-fry until the bits of egg have set. Give the mixture a good stir and turn on to a large platter. Garnish abundantly with the chives and serve at once.

97 Stir-fried Pasta with Orange and Curry

East meets West
Preparation time 20 minutes
Serves 4

450 g (1 lb) dried Italian pasta, such as fusilli or farfalle

3 tablespoons olive oil

3 tablespoons chopped garlic

1 tablespoon finely chopped fresh root ginger

1 small onion, chopped

2 tablespoons finely grated orange zest

6 bacon slices, chopped

2 red peppers (bell peppers), cut into 1 cm ($\frac{1}{2}$ inch) dice

2 yellow peppers (bell peppers), cut into 1 cm ($\frac{1}{2}$ inch) dice

2 teaspoons sugar

300 ml (10 fl oz) Chicken Stock (see page 134)

400 g (14 oz) ($1\frac{3}{4}$ cups) canned chopped tomatoes

3 tablespoons Madras curry paste

2 tablespoons tomato purée

1 teaspoon salt

$\frac{1}{2}$ teaspoon freshly ground black pepper

TO GARNISH:

a handful of fresh basil, chopped

a handful of fresh chives, snipped

One of the quickest and easiest ways to prepare Italian pasta is in the wok. I love using whatever leftovers I have in the refrigerator and quickly stir-frying cooked pasta with some curry paste. With a little imagination, the wok turns a simple pasta dish into an ambrosial delight. This recipe makes a fine appetizer or it can easily be a main course (entrée) with salad. In warm weather, serve at room temperature.

1 Cook the pasta in a large pan of boiling salted water until *al dente*, then drain well and set aside.

2 Heat a wok or large frying pan over a high heat and add the olive oil. When it is very hot and slightly smoking, add the garlic, ginger, onion and orange zest and stir-fry for 2 minutes. Then add the bacon and stir-fry for 3–4 minutes, until browned.

3 Add the peppers, sugar, stock, tomatoes, curry paste, tomato purée, salt and pepper. Reduce the heat, then cover and simmer for 30 minutes.

4 Add the drained pasta and mix well. Turn the mixture out on to a large warm platter, garnish generously with the basil and chives and serve at once.

98 Indonesian Fried Rice

Informal supper
Preparation time 30 minutes
Serves 4–6

enough basmati rice to fill a glass measuring jug to the 400 ml (14 fl oz) level (1¾ cups)

175 g (6 oz) raw prawns (green shrimp)

2 eggs, beaten

2 teaspoons sesame oil

1 teaspoon salt

2 tablespoons groundnut (peanut) oil

2 tablespoons coarsely chopped garlic

1 small onion, finely chopped

1 tablespoon shrimp paste

225 g (8 oz) minced (ground) pork or beef

1 tablespoon light soy sauce

2 teaspoons dark soy sauce

1 small cucumber, peeled and finely sliced

freshly ground black pepper

This is the famous *nasi goreng* – a truly delectable one-meal rice dish that is made simply in a wok. Unlike the Chinese version of fried rice, it includes a combination of meat and prawns. There is also the addition of soy sauce and shrimp paste, which is uniquely Indonesian. It is typical of the flavourful food one finds in Indonesia.

1 At least 2 hours in advance, or even the night before, cook the rice according to the instructions on page 135. Allow it to cool thoroughly and then refrigerate.

2 Peel the prawns, make a slit down the back of each one and pull out the fine digestive cord with the tip of the knife. Wash the prawns and pat them dry with kitchen paper, then cut them into 1 cm (½ inch) pieces.

3 Combine the eggs with the sesame oil, half the salt and some black pepper, then set aside.

4 Heat a wok or large frying pan over a high heat and add the groundnut oil. When it is very hot and slightly smoking, add the garlic, prawns, onion, shrimp paste, the remaining salt and some black pepper. Stir-fry for 2 minutes.

5 Add the minced pork or beef and stir-fry for 2 minutes, then add the rice and continue to stir-fry for 3 minutes. Next, add the light soy sauce and dark soy sauce and stir-fry for 2 minutes.

6 Add the egg mixture and stir-fry for another minute. Turn on to a platter, garnish with the sliced cucumber and serve.

99 Herbal Fried Rice

Light and fresh
Preparation time 15 minutes
Serves 4–6

enough basmati rice to fill a glass measuring jug to the 400 ml (14 fl oz) level (1¾ cups)

3 tablespoons extra virgin olive oil

3 tablespoons coarsely chopped garlic

2 teaspoons finely chopped fresh root ginger

2 teaspoons salt

1 teaspoon freshly ground black pepper

3 tablespoons finely chopped spring onions (scallions)

3 tablespoons finely chopped fresh chives

3 tablespoons finely chopped fresh coriander (cilantro)

1 tablespoon finely chopped fresh tarragon

2 teaspoons finely chopped fresh thyme

3 tablespoons finely chopped fresh parsley

3 tablespoons chopped fresh basil

Often when I cook at home, I have bits of all sorts of fresh herbs left over. I have found that using them with cooked rice is an economical, delicious and quick way not to waste them. The result is a wonderfully aromatic and fragrant rice dish.

1 At least 2 hours in advance, or even the night before, cook the rice according to the instructions on page 135. Allow it to cool thoroughly and then put it in the refrigerator.

2 Heat a wok or large frying pan and add the olive oil. Add the garlic and ginger and stir-fry for 15 seconds. Then add the cold rice, salt and pepper and stir-fry for 2 minutes over a high heat. Mix well, pressing on the cold rice to break up any lumps.

3 When the rice is heated through, add the spring onions and all the fresh herbs and stir-fry for 3 minutes. Transfer on to a serving platter and serve hot or at room temperature.

100 Sweetcorn and Ginger Fried Rice

East meets West
Preparation time 10 minutes
Serves 4

enough basmati rice to fill a glass measuring jug to the 400 ml (14 fl oz) level (1³/₄ cups)

450 g (1 lb) corn on the cob, or 275 g (10 oz) (1¹/₄ cups) canned sweetcorn

1 tablespoon groundnut (peanut) oil

1¹/₂ tablespoons finely chopped fresh root ginger

2 tablespoons finely chopped spring onions (scallions)

2 tablespoons Shaoxing rice wine or dry sherry

¹/₄ teaspoon salt

¹/₄ teaspoon freshly ground black pepper

2 tablespoons sesame oil

Sweetcorn and rice go well together, with their contrasting and complementary textures, colours and flavours. The addition of ginger makes them a little exotic – a true East–West delight. Use fresh corn if possible, and be sure the cooked rice is cold before stir-frying. This will prevent it absorbing too much oil and becoming sticky.

This economical and healthy dish may be eaten as a rice salad or as an accompaniment to other foods.

1 At least 2 hours in advance, or even the night before, cook the rice according to the instructions on page 135. Allow it to cool thoroughly and then put it in the refrigerator.

2 If using fresh corn, remove the kernels with a sharp knife or cleaver. You should end up with about 275 g (10 oz) (1¹/₄ cups) corn. If you are using canned corn, empty it into a sieve, drain well and set aside.

3 Heat a wok or large frying pan and add the groundnut oil. Put in the ginger and spring onions and stir-fry for a few seconds. Add the rice wine or sherry and stir-fry a few seconds longer.

4 Stir in the cold cooked rice and stir-fry for 5 minutes, then add the corn, salt and pepper and stir-fry for 2 minutes. Finally, add the sesame oil and stir-fry for a further 4 minutes until the corn is thoroughly cooked. Serve at once, or leave to cool and serve as a rice salad.

Chicken Stock

Makes 3.4 litres (6 UK pints)

2 kg (4½ lb) raw chicken bones, such as backs, feet, wings, etc.

675 g (1½ lb) chicken pieces, such as wings, thighs, drumsticks, etc.

3.4 litres (6 UK pints) cold water

3 slices of fresh root ginger

6 spring onions (scallions)

6 garlic cloves, unpeeled

1 teaspoon salt

1 Put the chicken bones and pieces into a large pot (the bones can be put in frozen, if necessary). Cover with the cold water and bring to a simmer. Meanwhile, slice the ginger diagonally into slices 5 x 1 cm (2 x ½ inch). Remove the green tops of the spring onions. Lightly crush the garlic cloves, leaving the skins on.

2 Using a large, flat spoon, skim off the scum as it rises from the bones. Watch the heat, as the stock should never boil. Keep skimming until the stock looks clear; this can take 20–40 minutes. Do not stir or disturb the stock.

3 Reduce the heat to a low simmer and add the ginger, spring onions, garlic and salt. Simmer the stock over a very low heat for 2–4 hours, skimming any fat from the top at least twice during this time. (The stock should be rich and full-bodied, which is why it needs to be simmered for such a long time. This way the stock – and any soup you make with it – will have plenty of flavour.)

4 Strain the stock through several layers of dampened muslin (cheesecloth) or through a very fine-meshed strainer, then let it cool completely. Remove any fat that has risen to the top. It is now ready to be used or transferred to containers and frozen for future use.

Fish Stock

Makes about 3.4 litres (6 UK pints)

2.75 kg (6 lb) fish bones from any firm-fleshed, white fish, such as halibut, sea bass, sole, monkfish or cod

3.4 litres (6 UK pints) cold water

225 g (8 oz) leeks

225 g (8 oz) (1 cup) chopped onions

450 g (1 lb) (2 cups) chopped carrots

1 Rinse the fish bones under cold running water until there is no sign of blood; the water should run clear. Put the bones in a very large pan, cover them with the cold water and bring to a simmer.

2 Meanwhile, trim the leeks and discard any yellow parts. Cut the leeks at the point where they begin to turn green and discard the green parts. Then split the white parts in half and rinse them well in cold running water until there is no trace of dirt. Coarsely chop the leeks.

3 Using a large, flat spoon, skim off the scum as it rises from the bones. Watch the heat, as the stock should never boil. Keep skimming until the stock looks clear; this can take 20–30 minutes. Do not stir or disturb the stock.

(continued opposite)

100 g (4 oz) (½ cup) chopped shallots

8 sprigs of fresh parsley

4 sprigs of fresh thyme or 2 teaspoons dried thyme

2 bay leaves

5 garlic cloves, unpeeled and lightly crushed

2 teaspoons salt

1 tablespoon black peppercorns

4 Now turn the heat down to a low simmer. Add the rest of the ingredients and simmer, uncovered, for 1 hour.

5 Remove the bones and other ingredients with a large, slotted spoon and strain the stock through several layers of dampened muslin (cheesecloth) or through a very fine-meshed strainer, then let it cool completely. It is now ready to be used or transferred to containers and frozen for future use.

Steamed Rice

This recipe serves 4
See method for ingredients

Steaming is a simple, direct and efficient cooking method for rice. I prefer to use Indian basmati or any other superior long-grain white rice, which will be dry and fluffy when cooked. Avoid pre-cooked or 'easy-cook' rice, as it lacks the full flavour and the texture of good long-grain rice.

The secret of preparing rice without it becoming sticky is to cook it first in an uncovered pan at a high heat until most of the water has evaporated. Then the heat should be turned very low, the pan covered, and the rice cooked slowly in the remaining steam. Never uncover the pan once the steaming process has begun; just time it and wait. Here is a good trick to remember: if you cover the rice with about 2.5 cm (1 inch) of water, it should always cook properly without sticking. Many packet recipes for rice use too much water, resulting in a gluey mess.

1 Measure the long-grain rice in a jug to the 400 ml (14 fl oz) level (1¾ cups). Put the rice in a large bowl and wash it in several changes of water until the water becomes clear.

2 Drain the rice, put it into a heavy pan with 600 ml (1 UK pint) water and bring to the boil. Boil, uncovered, for about 5 minutes, until most of the surface liquid has evaporated. The surface of the rice should have small indentations like a pitted crater. At this point, cover the pan with a very tight-fitting lid, turn the heat as low as possible and let the rice cook undisturbed for 15 minutes.

3 There is no need to 'fluff' the rice; just let it rest off the heat for 5 minutes before serving.

Garlic, Ginger and Spring Onion Oil

Makes 300 ml (10 fl oz)

300 ml (10 fl oz) groundnut
(peanut) or vegetable oil

6 tablespoons thinly sliced garlic

12 slices of fresh root ginger,
5 x 1 cm (2 x ½ inch)

6 spring onions (scallions)

1 Heat a wok or large frying pan over a high heat and add the oil. When it is very hot and slightly smoking, add the garlic, ginger and spring onions. Cook until the vegetables turn brown, then remove from the heat immediately and allow to cool thoroughly. Leave to stand overnight.

2 Strain the mixture through a fine sieve. Use at once or store, tightly covered, in the refrigerator, for up to 6 months. Bring to room temperature before using.

Chive-flavoured Olive Oil

Makes 400 ml (14 fl oz)

about 4 x 100 g (4 oz) bunches
of fresh chives,

2 tablespoons water

300 ml (10 fl oz) extra virgin
olive oil

1 Put the chives in a juice extractor, blender or food processor, with the water, and extract the juice. Strain through a fine sieve, if using a blender or processor. You should have about 135 ml (4 ½ fl oz) juice.

2 Combine the chive juice with the olive oil in a blender and mix well. Use at once or store, tightly covered, in the refrigerator for up to 3 days. Bring to room temperature and shake before using.

Curry-flavoured Oil

Makes 300 ml (10 fl oz)

300 ml (10 fl oz) groundnut
(peanut) or vegetable oil

6 tablespoons Madras curry
powder

1 Heat a wok or large frying pan over a high heat and add the oil. When it is very hot and slightly smoking, remove from the heat, add the curry powder and stir to mix well. Allow the mixture to cool thoroughly and leave to stand overnight.

2 Strain the mixture through a fine sieve. Use at once or store, tightly covered, in the refrigerator for up to 6 months. Bring to room temperature before using.

Chilli Oil (Chilli Dipping Sauce)

Makes 300 ml (10 fl oz)

300 ml (10 fl oz) groundnut (peanut) oil

2 tablespoons dried red chilli peppers, including seeds, coarsely chopped

1 tablespoon whole, unroasted Sichuan peppercorns (see page 140)

2 tablespoons whole black beans, rinsed and dried

1 Heat a wok or large frying pan until it is very hot. Add the oil and, when it is very hot and slightly smoking, turn the heat to low. Add the chilli peppers, peppercorns and black beans and cook gently for about 15 minutes.

2 Allow the mixture to cool undisturbed, then pour it into a jar. Leave it to stand for 2 days then strain the oil. It will keep indefinitely.

Sweet Chilli Sauce

Makes 300 ml (10 fl oz)

175 g (6 oz) (about 2) large, fresh red chilli peppers, finely chopped (deseeded first if you prefer a milder flavour)

3 tablespoons coarsely chopped garlic

1 tablespoon sugar

1 tablespoon white rice vinegar or malt vinegar

1 tablespoon fish sauce (*nam pla*)

1 tablespoon vegetable oil

150 ml (5 fl oz) water

salt

1 Put all the ingredients in a wok or saucepan and bring to the boil. Turn the heat very low, then cover and simmer gently for 15 minutes. Remove from the heat and leave to cool.

2 Purée the mixture in a blender or food processor until it is a smooth paste. Re-heat in a wok or saucepan for about 3 minutes to bring out the flavour, adding more salt if necessary. Once cool, it is ready to use or can be stored in the refrigerator.

Ingredients

Beancurd (Tofu)

You will need the solid form of beancurd for stir-frying. Beancurd 'cakes' are white in colour and are sold in supermarkets, Chinese grocer's and healthfood shops. They are packed in water in plastic containers and may be kept in this state in the refrigerator for up to 5 days, provided the water is changed daily. To use solid beancurd, cut it into cubes or shreds with a sharp knife. Do this with care, as it is delicate. It also needs to be cooked carefully, as too much stirring can cause it to crumble.

Black beans

These small, black soya beans are preserved by being fermented with salt and spices, giving them a distinctive, slightly salty taste and a pleasant, rich smell. They make a tasty seasoning, especially when used in conjunction with garlic or fresh ginger. They are inexpensive and can be obtained from Chinese grocers, usually in cans labelled 'black beans in salted sauce'. Rinse them before use; I prefer to chop them slightly, too, as it helps to release their pungent flavour. If you transfer any unused beans and liquid to a sealed jar, they will keep indefinitely in the refrigerator.

Chilli bean sauce

This thick, dark sauce or paste is made from soya beans, chilli peppers and other seasonings, and is very hot and spicy. Be sure to seal the jar tightly after use and store in the larder or refrigerator. Do not confuse it with chilli sauce, which is a hotter, redder, thinner condiment made without beans.

Chilli peppers

Fresh chilli peppers

To prepare fresh chilli peppers, rinse them in cold water, then slit them lengthways with a small, sharp knife. Remove and discard the seeds. Rinse the chilli peppers again under cold running water and then prepare them according to the recipe. Wash your hands, knife and chopping board before preparing other foods, and be careful not to touch your eyes until you have washed your hands thoroughly.

Dried red chilli peppers

The dried red chilli peppers used in China are usually small, thin and about 1 cm (½ inch) long. They are normally left whole or cut in half lengthways with the seeds left in and used to season oil. They can be found in oriental shops and most supermarkets and will keep indefinitely in a sealed jar.

Chilli powder

Chilli powder is made from dried red chilli peppers and is used in many spicy dishes. As with chilli peppers in general, add it according to taste.

Chinese dried mushrooms

There are many varieties of these, either black or brown, but the very large, pale ones with a cracked surface are the best. They are available in boxes or plastic bags from Chinese grocers. Store in an airtight jar.

To use dried mushrooms, soak them in a bowl of warm water for about 20 minutes, until they are soft and pliable. Squeeze out the excess water, then cut off and discard the woody stems. Only the caps should be used. The soaking water can be strained and saved for use in soups and cooking rice.

Citrus peel

Dried citrus peel, made from tangerines or oranges, is used extensively in Chinese cookery to flavour braised and smoked dishes. The peel also adds an intense aroma and taste to stir-fried dishes. Drying the peel concentrates the flavour, but you can use the same quantity of fresh peel if necessary.

Chinese dried citrus peel can be found in Chinese grocer's shops; however, it is simple to make your own. Peel the skin off a tangerine or orange, scraping away as much of the white parts as possible, or coarsely grate the skin. Lay the peel on kitchen paper and dry it in the sun, in an airing cupboard or in a warm but unlit oven, until it is dry and hard. Store in a tightly sealed container in a cool, dry place.

To use dried citrus peel, soak it in warm water until it softens, then chop or slice it according to the recipe. Add grated peel without soaking it first.

Cloud ears

These tiny, black, dried leaves are also known as Chinese tree fungus. They are valued for their crunchy texture and slightly smoky flavour. You should be able to find them at Chinese markets, usually wrapped in plastic bags. They keep indefinitely in a jar stored in a cool, dry place. Before use, soak them in hot water for 20–30 minutes until soft, then rinse well, cutting away any hard bits.

Fish sauce

Fish sauce, or *nam pla*, is also known as fish gravy. It is a thin, brown liquid made from fermented salted fish, usually anchovies, and has a noticeably fishy odour and salty taste. The Thai brands are especially good, with a less salty taste. Fish sauce is an inexpensive ingredient, so buy the best on offer.

Garlic

Select bulbs of garlic that are firm and preferably pinkish in colour. Store garlic in a cool, dry place but not in the refrigerator, where it can easily become mildewed or start sprouting.

Ginger

Select firm, unshrivelled pieces and peel off the skin before use. It will keep for about 2 weeks if well wrapped in cling film (plastic wrap) in the refrigerator. Most of the recipes in this book that require ginger specify that it should be finely shredded or chopped. For shredded ginger, thinly slice a piece lengthways, then stack and cut lengthways again into fine strips. To chop finely, turn the shredded ginger round and chop it horizontally.

Hoisin sauce

This thick, dark, brownish-red sauce, made from soya beans, vinegar, sugar, spices and other flavourings, is sweet and spicy.

It is sold in cans and jars (sometimes labelled as barbecue sauce) and is available in Chinese shops and many supermarkets. If refrigerated, it should keep indefinitely.

Noodles

Bean thread (transparent noodles)

Also called cellophane noodles, these very fine, white noodles are made from ground mung beans. They are available dried, packed in neat, plastic-wrapped bundles, from Chinese shops.

Rice noodles

These dried noodles are opaque white and come in a variety of shapes and thicknesses. Rice noodles are easy to prepare: simply soak them in warm water for 20 minutes until they are soft, then drain in a colander or sieve. They are now ready to be used in stir-fries or soups.

Wheat noodles and egg noodles

Available dried or fresh, these are made from hard or soft wheat flour, water, and sometimes egg, in which case they are labelled egg noodles. Rounded ones are best for frying. If you are cooking noodles ahead of time or before stir-frying them, toss the cooked, drained noodles in 2 teaspoons of sesame oil and put them into a bowl. Cover with cling film (plastic wrap) and refrigerate for up to 2 hours.

Oils

Groundnut (Peanut) oil

This is also known as arachide oil. I prefer to use it for Asian cookery because it has a pleasant, unobtrusive taste. Although it has a higher saturated fat content than some oils, its ability to be heated to a high temperature without burning makes it perfect for stir-frying. If you cannot find it, use corn oil instead.

Sesame oil

This thick, rich, golden-brown oil made from sesame seeds has a distinctive, nutty flavour and aroma. It is widely used in Chinese cookery as a seasoning but is not normally used as a cooking oil because it burns easily. Think of it more as a flavouring. A small amount is often added at the last moment to finish a dish.

Oyster sauce

This thick, brown sauce is made from a concentrate of oysters cooked in soy sauce and brine. Despite its name, it does not taste fishy. It is usually sold in bottles and can be bought in supermarkets. I find it keeps best in the refrigerator. A vegetarian 'oyster' sauce made with mushrooms is now available.

Peanuts

The thin, red skins of raw peanuts should be removed before use. To do this, simply immerse the nuts in a pan of boiling water for about 2 minutes, then drain and leave to cool; the skins will come off easily.

Prawns (Shrimp)

For most of the recipes in this book you will need medium-to-large raw, unshelled prawns. These are sweeter and more succulent than ready-cooked ones. Before cooking, they should be shelled and, if large, de-veined. To remove the shell, twist off the head and discard, then, using your fingers, break open the shell along the belly and peel it off. Run a small, sharp knife along the back of the prawn and pull out the dark intestinal vein. The tail shell can be left on for presentation.

Shaoxing rice wine

Rice wine is used extensively for cooking and drinking throughout China, but I believe the finest of its many varieties is from Shaoxing, in Zhejiang Province in eastern China. It is made from glutinous rice, yeast and spring water. Now readily available in the West in Chinese markets and some liquor stores, it should be kept tightly corked and at room temperature.

A good-quality, pale, dry sherry can be substituted but cannot match its rich, mellow taste.

Shrimp paste

This is made from pulverized salted shrimp that has been left to ferment. The mixture is dried in the sun and cut into cakes. Although shrimp paste smells very assertive, remember that the cooking process quickly tames its aroma and taste. It is available in both Thai and Chinese food shops but the best brands come from Thailand. Shrimp paste will last indefinitely if stored, wrapped, in the refrigerator.

Sichuan peppercorns

Sichuan peppercorns are reddish-brown in colour and have a pungent odour that distinguishes them from the hotter black peppercorns. They don't actually come from peppers at all, but are the dried berries of a shrub that is a member of the citrus family. They are inexpensive and sold wrapped in cellophane or plastic bags in Chinese grocer's shops. They will keep indefinitely if stored in a well-sealed container.

To roast Sichuan peppercorns, heat a wok or heavy frying pan to a medium heat. Add the peppercorns (you can roast about 150 g/5 oz ($2/3$ cup) at a time) and stir-fry for about 5 minutes, until they brown slightly and start to smoke. Remove from the heat and let them cool. Grind the peppercorns in a pepper mill or with a mortar and pestle. Keep the mixture tightly sealed in a screw-top jar. Alternatively, keep the whole roasted peppercorns in a well-sealed container and grind them when required. Please note that Sichuan peppercorns are not available in America. Instead, you can substitute half the quantity with black peppercorns and the remaining half with aniseed.

Soy sauce

Soy sauce is made from a mixture of soya beans, flour and water, which is then fermented naturally and aged for some months. The liquid that is finally distilled is soy sauce.

There are two main types. Light soy sauce, as the name implies, is light in colour, but it is full of flavour and is the better one to use for cooking. It is saltier than dark soy sauce, and is known in Chinese grocer's shops as Superior Soy. Dark soy sauce, confusingly, is known as Soy Superior Sauce. It is aged for much longer than light soy sauce, hence its darker, almost black colour, and is also slightly thicker and stronger.

Spring onions (Scallions)

The recipes in this book specify a variety of ways to prepare spring onions (scallions or green onions) for cooking and for garnish. First, peel off the outer layer if it is bruised or damaged. Trim the tops and bottoms and remove any damaged green tops. Rinse well to remove any dirt. To chop finely, split into quarters lengthways, then chop into small pieces horizontally. To shred, cut the onions in half horizontally, then split very finely lengthways.

Vinegar

Vinegars are widely used in Chinese cooking. Unlike Western vinegars, they are usually made from rice. There are many varieties, ranging in flavour from the spicy and slightly tart to the sweet and pungent. All these vinegars can be bought in Chinese grocers and will keep indefinitely. If you cannot get Chinese vinegars, I suggest you use cider vinegar. Malt vinegar can be used, but its taste is stronger and more acidic.

White rice vinegar

White rice vinegar is clear and mild in flavour. It has a faint taste of glutinous rice and is used for sweet-and-sour dishes.

Black rice vinegar

Black rice vinegar is very dark in colour and rich, though mild, in taste. It is used for braised dishes, sauces, and sometimes as a dipping sauce for crab.

Red rice vinegar

Red rice vinegar is sweet and spicy in taste and is often used as a dipping sauce for seafood.

Water chestnuts

Water chestnuts are white, sweet, crunchy bulbs about the size of a walnut. They are sold in cans in many supermarkets and have a good texture but little taste. Rinse them well in cold water before use and store any unused ones in a jar of water. They will keep for several weeks in the refrigerator if you change the water daily.

Index

Page numbers in *italics* refer to illustrations

A

angel hair pasta with spicy tomato sauce 124, *125*
asparagus
    asparagus in black bean sauce 90, *91*
    Indonesian-style chicken with vegetables *58*, 59
savoury beef with asparagus 15
aubergines (eggplant)
    stir-fried vegetables over a rice noodle cloud
       116, 117
    Thai green curry chicken with aubergines 60

B

bacon
    stir-fried fusilli *alla carbonara* *126*, 127
    stir-fried pasta with orange and curry 128
basil
    chicken with chillies and basil 52, *53*
    spicy pork with fragrant basil 24, *25*
    squid with chilli and basil 83
    Thai-style duck 62, *63*
bean sprouts
    stir-fried rice noodles 123
bean thread noodles 139
    Korean bean thread sesame noodles and
       vegetables 122
beancurd (tofu) 138
    quick beancurd in spicy chilli sauce 88
    spicy orange-flavoured beancurd 113
beef
    beef in oyster sauce 12
    beef with five peppercorns 10, *11*
    beef with ginger and pineapple 14
    beef with orange 22
    fragrant beef with peppers 16, *17*
    savoury beef with asparagus 15
    stir-fried curry beef 13
    Thai-style chilli beef 19
    Vietnamese-style lemongrass beef *20*, 21
    warm Vietnamese beef salad 18
bell peppers *see* peppers
black beans 138
    asparagus in black bean sauce 90, *91*
    chicken with black bean sauce 50
    fish with black bean sauce 86
    hot pepper prawns (shrimp) 71
    mussels in black bean sauce 80–2
    prawns (shrimp) and scallops in black bean
       and tomato butter sauce 72, *73*
broad beans with red curry *100*, 101
broccoli
    broccoli chicken 48
    Hong Kong-style broccoli and baby corn *94*, 95
    Indonesian-style chicken with vegetables *58*, 59

C

cabbage, hot and spicy stir-fried 92

carrots, ginger-garlic 96, *97*
cashews, stir-fried chilli pork with 28, *29*
cauliflower with fresh coriander (cilantro) 93
celery
    cloud ears stir-fried with mangetout (snow-
      peas) *106*, 107
chicken
    broccoli chicken 48
    chicken stock 134
    chicken with black bean sauce 50
    chicken with chillies and basil 52, *53*
    chicken with Chinese and button mushrooms 56
    chow mein 115
    five-spice chicken 55
    garlic chicken with cucumber 40
    Indonesian-style chicken with vegetables *58*, 59
    lemon chicken 41
    pineapple chicken 61
    quick orange and lemon chicken 51
    shredded chicken with sesame seeds 46, *47*
    smoked chicken 54
    spicy chicken with mint 44
    stir-fried chicken with grilled peppers *42*, 43
    Thai green curry chicken with aubergines
      (eggplant) 60
    Thai-style ginger chicken 49
    Vietnamese-style lemongrass chicken 57
    walnut chicken 45
chicken livers with onions 54–5
chilli bean sauce 138
    Hunan-style lamb 35
    quick beancurd (tofu) in spicy chilli sauce 88
    spicy courgettes (zucchini) 88–9
    stir-fried chilli pork with cashews 28, *29*
chilli peppers *see* chillies
chilli powder 138
chillies (chilli peppers) 138
    beef with orange 22
    chicken with chillies and basil 52, *53*
    chilli oil (chilli dipping sauce) 137
    five-spice chicken 55
    garlic scallops 77
    hot pepper prawns (shrimp) 71
    Indonesian-style chicken with vegetables *58*, 59
    pork with shrimp paste 26
    Singapore noodles 120–1
    spicy orange-flavoured beancurd (tofu) 113
    squid with chilli and basil 83
    stir-fried pork with mushrooms *32*, 33
    stir-fried rice noodles 123
    sweet chilli sauce 137
    Thai-style chilli beef 19
    Thai-style duck 62, *63*
    Vietnamese-style lemongrass beef *20*, 21
    Vietnamese-style lemongrass chicken 57
Chinese cabbage *see* Chinese leaves

Chinese leaves (Chinese cabbage)
    smoked chicken 54
    stir-fried Chinese greens 99
chive-flavoured olive oil 136
chopsticks 8
chow mein 115
cilantro *see* coriander
citrus peel 138–9
cleaning woks 8
cleavers 8–9
cloud ears 139
    cloud ears stir-fried with mangetout (snow-
      peas) *106*, 107
coconut milk
    green Thai curry mussels 80, *81*
cod
    fish with black bean sauce 86
    fish with peas 87
coriander (cilantro)
    cauliflower with fresh coriander (cilantro) 93
corn
    eggs and corn with spring onions (scallions)
      and ginger 89
    Hong Kong-style broccoli and baby corn *94*, 95
    sweetcorn and ginger fried rice *132*, 133
courgettes (zucchini)
    mock vegetable pasta 112
    spicy courgettes 88–9
    stir-fried vegetables over a rice noodle cloud
      116, 117
cucumber
    cucumber with hot spices 98
    garlic chicken with cucumber 40
curries
    broad beans with red curry *100*, 101
    curry-flavoured oil 136
    green Thai curry mussels 80, *81*
    quick curry noodles 121
    stir-fried curry beef 13
    stir-fried pasta with orange and curry 128
    Thai green curry chicken with aubergines
      (eggplant) 60

D

duck, Thai-style 62, *63*

E

eggplant *see* aubergine
egg noodles 139–40
    chow mein 115
    spicy Sichuan noodles 118, *119*
eggs
    eggs and corn with spring onions (scallions)
      and ginger 89
    prawns (shrimp) with egg 68
    Singapore noodles 120–1
    stir-fried fusilli *alla carbonara* *126*, 127
equipment 7–9

F
fennel with garlic 99
fish
    fish stock 134–5
    fish with black bean sauce 86
    fish with peas 87
fish sauce 139
    broccoli chicken 48
five-spice powder
    five-spice chicken 55
    stir-fried five-spice vegetables 109
fragrant beef with peppers 16, *17*
French beans
    bright pepper and green bean stir-fry 102, *103*
fusilli
    stir-fried fusilli *alla carbonara 126*, 127
    stir-fried pasta with orange and curry 128
G
garlic 139
    fennel with garlic 99
    garlic chicken with cucumber 40
    garlic, ginger and spring onion (scallion) oil 136
    garlic scallops 77
    ginger-garlic carrots 96, *97*
    Hunan-style lamb 35
    lamb with garlic 38
    spinach with garlic 102
    stir-fried garlic pork 23
    stir-fried mushrooms Provençal 108
    stir-fried *persillade* prawns (shrimp) *66, 67*
ginger 139
    beef with ginger and pineapple 14
    eggs and corn with spring onions (scallions) and ginger 89
    garlic, ginger and spring onion (scallion) oil 136
    ginger-garlic carrots 96, *97*
    prawns (shrimp) in ginger sauce 74
    sweetcorn and ginger fried rice *132, 133*
    Thai-style ginger chicken 49
groundnut oil (peanut oil) 140
H
ham
    chow mein 115
    fish with peas 87
herbal fried rice 130, *131*
hoisin sauce 139
    Hunan-style lamb 35
    stir-fried hoisin turnips 96
Hong Kong-style broccoli and baby corn *94, 95*
hot and sour Indonesian prawns (shrimp) 65
hot and spicy stir-fried cabbage 92
hot and tangy minced (ground) lamb 39
hot pepper prawns (shrimp) 71
Hunan-style lamb 35
I
Indonesian fried rice 129
Indonesian-style chicken with vegetables *58, 59*
ingredients 138–41
K
Korean bean thread sesame noodles and vegetables 122
L
lamb
    hot and tangy minced (ground) lamb 39

Hunan-style lamb 35
    lamb with garlic 38
    spicy orange lamb 36, *37*
lemon
    lemon chicken 41
    quick orange and lemon chicken 51
    salmon with lemon *84, 85*
lemongrass
    fragrant beef with peppers 16, *17*
    Vietnamese-style lemongrass beef *20*, 21
    Vietnamese-style lemongrass chicken 57
liver
    chicken livers with onions 54–5
lychees, stir-fried pork with 31
M
mangetout (snowpeas)
    chow mein 115
    cloud ears stir-fried with mangetout (snow peas) *106, 107*
mango prawns (shrimp) 64
mint, spicy chicken with 44
mock vegetable pasta 112
mushrooms 138
    chicken with Chinese and button mushrooms 56
    cloud ears stir-fried with mangetout (snow peas) *106, 107*
    Indonesian-style chicken with vegetables *58, 59*
    spicy stir-fried mushrooms 105
    stir-fried mushrooms Provençal 108
    stir-fried pork with mushrooms *32, 33*
mussels
    green Thai curry mussels 80, *81*
    mussels in black bean sauce 80–2
N
Napa cabbage *see* Chinese leaves
noodles 139–40
    chow mein 115
    Korean bean thread sesame noodles and vegetables 122
    quick curry noodles 121
    Singapore noodles 120–1
    spicy Sichuan noodles 118, *119*
    stir-fried rice noodles 123
    stir-fried vegetables over a rice noodle cloud *116*, 117
O
oils 140
    chilli oil (chilli dipping sauce) 137
    chive-flavoured olive oil 136
    curry-flavoured oil 136
    garlic, ginger and spring onion (scallion) oil 136
onions
    chicken livers with onions 54–5
    spicy orange-flavoured beancurd (tofu) 113
    stir-fried curry beef 13
orange
    beef with orange 22
    orange peel 138–9
    quick orange and lemon chicken 51
    spicy orange-flavoured beancurd (tofu) 113
    spicy orange lamb 36, *37*
    stir-fried pasta with orange and curry 128
oyster sauce 140
    beef in oyster sauce 12

    broccoli chicken 48
P
Pak choy *see* Chinese leaves
pancetta
    stir-fried fusilli *alla carbonara* 126, 127
Parma ham
    chow mein 115
    fish with peas 87
parsley
    stir-fried mushrooms Provençal 108
    stir-fried *persillade* prawns (shrimp) 66, 67
pasta
    angel hair pasta with spicy tomato sauce 124, *125*
    stir-fried fusilli *alla carbonara* 126, 127
    stir fried pasta with orange and curry 128
peanut oil (groundnut oil) 140
peanuts 140
    Sichuan-style pork with peanuts 30
    Vietnamese-style lemongrass chicken 57
peas
    fish with peas 87
    prawns (shrimp) with water chestnuts 75
    Singapore noodles 120–1
    squid with chilli and basil 83
Peking cabbage *see* Chinese leaves
peppercorns
    beef with five peppercorns 10, *11*
    Sichuan peppercorns 140–1
peppers (bell peppers)
    beef with ginger and pineapple 14
    bright pepper and green bean stir-fry 102, *103*
    fennel with garlic 99
    fragrant beef with peppers 16, *17*
    spicy chicken with mint 44
    stir-fried chicken with grilled peppers *42, 43*
    stir-fried pasta with orange and curry 128
    sweet and sour prawns (shrimp) 69
persillade prawns (shrimp) 66, 67
petits pois
    squid with chilli and basil 83
pineapple
    beef with ginger and pineapple 14
    pineapple chicken 61
pork
    Indonesian fried rice 129
    pork with shrimp paste 26
    prawn and pork stir-fry 70
    Sichuan-style pork with peanuts 30
    Singapore noodles 120–1
    spicy pork with fragrant basil 24, *25*
    spicy Sichuan noodles 118, *119*
    stir-fried chilli pork with cashews 28, *29*
    stir-fried garlic pork 23
    stir-fried pork with lychees 31
    stir-fried pork with mushrooms *32, 33*
    stir-fried pork with spinach 34
    stir-fried pork with spring onions (scallions) 27
prawns (shrimp) 140
    hot and sour Indonesian prawns 65
    hot pepper prawns 71
    Indonesian fried rice 129
    mango prawns 64
    prawn and pork stir-fry 70

prawns and scallops in black bean and tomato butter sauce 72, *73*
prawns in ginger sauce 74
prawns with egg 68
prawns with water chestnuts 75
Singapore noodles 120–1
stir-fried *persillade* prawns *66, 67*
stir-fried rice noodles 123
sweet and sour prawns 69

Q
quick beancurd (tofu) in spicy chilli sauce 88
quick curry noodles 121
quick orange and lemon chicken 51

R
rainbow vegetables 110, *111*
rice
    herbal fried rice 130, *131*
    Indonesian fried rice 129
    steamed rice 135
    sweetcorn and ginger fried rice *132*, 133
rice noodles 139
    Singapore noodles 120–1
    stir-fried rice noodles 123
    stir-fried vegetables over a rice noodle cloud *116*, 117
rice vinegar 141
rice wine, Shaoxing 140

S
salad, warm Vietnamese beef 18
salmon
    salmon with lemon *84*, 85
    spicy salmon 82
sauce, sweet chilli 137
savoury beef with asparagus 15
scallions *see* spring onions
scallops
    garlic scallops 77
    prawns (shrimp) and scallops in black bean and tomato butter sauce 72, *73*
    Sichuan-style scallops 76
    spicy scallops with sun-dried tomatoes *78, 79*
seasoning woks 8
sesame oil 140
sesame seeds, shredded chicken with 46, *47*

Shaoxing rice wine 140
shredded chicken with sesame seeds 46, *47*
shrimp *see* prawns
shrimp paste 140
    pork with shrimp paste 26
Sichuan peppercorns 140–1
Sichuan-style pork with peanuts 30
Sichuan-style scallops 76
Singapore noodles 120–1
smoked chicken 54
snowpeas *see* mangetout
soy sauce 141
spatulas 9
spicy chicken with mint 44
spicy courgettes (zucchini) 88–9
spicy orange-flavoured beancurd (tofu) 113
spicy orange lamb 36, *37*
spicy pork with fragrant basil 24, *25*
spicy salmon 82
spicy scallops with sun-dried tomatoes *78, 79*
spicy Sichuan noodles 118, *119*
spicy stir-fried mushrooms 105
spinach
    spinach with garlic 102
    stir-fried pork with spinach 34
    stir-fried Singapore water spinach 104
spring onions (scallions) 141
    eggs and corn with spring onions and ginger 89
    garlic, ginger and spring onion oil 136
    stir-fried pork with spring onions 27
squid with chilli and basil 83
steamed rice 135
stocks
    chicken stock 134
    fish stock 134–5
sweet and sour prawns (shrimp) 69
sweet chilli sauce 137
sweetcorn
    eggs and corn with spring onions (scallions) and ginger 89
    Indonesian-style chicken with vegetables *58*, 59
    sweetcorn and ginger fried rice *132*, 133

T
Thai fish sauce 139

broccoli chicken 48
Thai green curry chicken with aubergines (eggplant) 60
Thai-style chilli beef 19
Thai-style duck 62, *63*
Thai-style ginger chicken 49
Tofu *see* beancurd
tomatoes
    angel hair pasta with spicy tomato sauce 124, *125*
    broccoli chicken 48
    prawns (shrimp) and scallops in black bean and tomato butter sauce 72, *73*
    spicy scallops with sun-dried tomatoes *78, 79*
    stir-fried pasta with orange and curry 128
turnips, stir-fried hoisin 96

V
vegetables
    Korean bean thread sesame noodles and vegetables 122
    rainbow vegetables 110, *111*
    stir-fried five-spice vegetables 109
    stir-fried mixed vegetables 114
    see also individual types of vegetable
Vietnamese beef salad 18
Vietnamese-style lemongrass beef *20*, 21
Vietnamese-style lemongrass chicken 57
vinegar 141

W
walnut chicken 45
water chestnuts 141
    cloud ears stir-fried with mangetout (snow peas) *106*, 107
    prawns (shrimp) with water chestnuts 75
    Singapore noodles 120–1
    sweet and sour prawns (shrimp) 69
water spinach, stir-fried Singapore 104
wheat noodles 139–40
wine, Shaoxing rice 140
woks 7–8

Z
zucchini *see* courgettes

Food photography by Steve Lee

Published by BBC Books, BBC Worldwide Ltd, 80 Wood Lane, London W12 0TT

First published 2004
© Promo Group Limited 2004
The moral right of the author has been asserted

Food photography © BBC Worldwide 2004

ISBN 0 563 52164 3

Commissioning Editor: Vivien Bowler
Project Editors: Sarah Lavelle and Dee O'Reilly
Copy-editor: Jane Middleton
Cover Art Director: Pene Parker
Book Designer: Lisa Pettibone
Food Stylist: Joss Herd
Stylist: Wei Tang
Production Controller: Arlene Alexander

Set in Caecilia and Foundry Sans
Printed and bound in France by Imprimerie Pollina
Colour separations by Radstock Reproductions Ltd, Midsomer Norton

If you require further information on any BBC Worldwide product call 08700 777 001 or visit our website on *www.bbcshop.com*

The Publishers would like to thank Westmill Foods for supplying two portraits of Ken Hom (on the cover and on page 6). Photos © Westmill Foods. Courtesy of *Ken Hom cooks...*, Ken's range of Oriental sauces, rice and noodles.

If you would like details of Ken Hom's range of woks and accessories, please contact:
Consumer Services, William Levene Ltd
Bridge House, Eelmoor Road
Farnborough GU14 7UE, UK
Tel: +44 1252 522 322
Fax: +44 1252 522 542

www.kenhom.com

19.95